Andrea!
I love you!

Thank you
for helping make
EVOLKMKD what
it is.

Love,
    Meg

"As a writer of business books, I know how much we can learn from reading about the journeys of successful entrepreneurs. And what a journey Megan Driscoll recounts in her wonderful new book, *#Resolve to Evolve*. From the time I covered Evolve's 'Family Night' in my *USA Today* column, I have followed her company's growth and been impressed that even with such fast and impressive growth, she has managed to keep true to the personal touch that keeps clients coming back, which accounts for almost all of her business coming from word of mouth. This book is a great example of how relationships—and a lot of hard work—can build a company. A must read for entrepreneurs and aspiring entrepreneurs, especially women!"

—RHONDA ABRAMS, USA Today *business columnist and author of* Successful Business Plans: Secrets & Strategies

"Anyone who has a sense of purpose to their work (or is currently grasping for one) will resonate with Megan's drive to 'make a real difference in the real lives of real people.' And anyone looking to start their own business, in particular, will be furiously taking notes about how to build an efficient, happy, and effective team. Megan has been a longtime mentor of mine, and her book reads like a blueprint of the years of over-dinner conversations we've had about the secrets of success. All the wisdom she's picked up in the public relations business is quickly applicable to the entrepreneur in all of us: honesty first, prioritize your internal team, don't skimp on the experts that support you, and—my favorite catchphrase of Megan's—'Be kind—don't suck.' Ultimately, *#Resolve to Evolve* is about how to do the work you love so effectively that you can also—gasp!—have a life. I don't know anyone who isn't interested in perfecting that balance."

—**KATIE BECKER**, *beauty and health director,* ELLE

"Megan Driscoll and the team at EvolveMKD are the best public relations, communications, and social media company that I've worked with. They work to support my business objectives and deliverables as if they are their own. If they say something will get done, it will get done and on time. The team has always delivered for my brands. Moreover, Megan is a true confidant and is an incredibly valuable resource well beyond her firm's swim lane. I am a better professional and leader with her support and counsel."

—**ROB CATLIN**, *vice president, Aesthetic Sales and Marketing, Endo Pharmaceuticals*

"Invest the time to meet a mythical unicorn who has built a business based upon values, ethics, and a frankness about how 'not every work problem is fixable.' Megan Driscoll takes us through a journey of what it means to start a business, recover from failure, stumble with simple things, and thrive under the pressure of competing in the agency world. She shares great stories of hiring successes, client disasters, moments of self-reflection that will make every reader think twice about their own choices, and how living your passion can make good business sense."

—JOY E. TAYLOR, *principal, Grant Thornton; former CEO, TayganPoint Consulting Group*

"I've watched Megan Driscoll and her team at EvolveMKD build a dynamic and thoughtful business since becoming her friend in 2016. As an entrepreneur myself, I've been impressed at how Meg and her team have maintained the 'family' feel of the agency, even while doubling the business in a short time period. This book is a phenomenal asset for anyone looking for an honest and real depiction of the challenges of growing and running a client service business while staying on the cutting edge of the latest and greatest marketing, communications, and digital trends."

—BARBARA ROBERTS, *entrepreneur in residence, Columbia and Hofstra Universities; former CEO, FPG International and Acoustiguide*

#RESOLVE
TO EVOLVE

MEGAN DRISCOLL

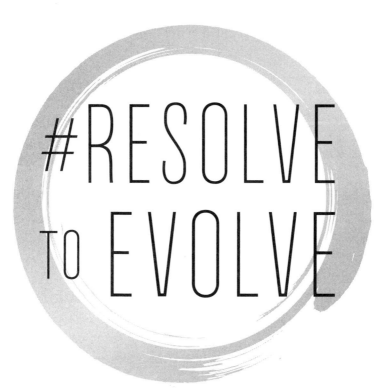

#RESOLVE TO EVOLVE

HOW BEING **PERSONAL** ABOUT BUSINESS CAN HELP IT **GROW**

ForbesBooks

Published by ForbesBooks, Charleston, South Carolina.
Member of Advantage Media Group.

ForbesBooks is a registered trademark, and the ForbesBooks colophon is a trademark of Forbes Media, LLC.

Printed in the United States of America.

10 9 8 7 6 5 4 3 2 1

ISBN: 978-1-94663-335-4
LCCN: 2019915817

Book design by Carly Blake.

This publication is designed to provide accurate and authoritative information in regard to the subject matter covered. It is sold with the understanding that the publisher is not engaged in rendering legal, accounting, or other professional services. If legal advice or other expert assistance is required, the services of a competent professional person should be sought.

Advantage Media Group is proud to be a part of the Tree Neutral® program. Tree Neutral offsets the number of trees consumed in the production and printing of this book by taking proactive steps such as planting trees in direct proportion to the number of trees used to print books. To learn more about Tree Neutral, please visit **www.treeneutral.com**.

Since 1917, the Forbes mission has remained constant. Global Champions of Entrepreneurial Capitalism. ForbesBooks exists to further that aim by bringing the Stories, Passion, and Knowledge of top thought leaders to the forefront. ForbesBooks brings you The Best in Business. To be considered for publication, please visit **www.forbesbooks.com**.

To #hothusband, who makes all things possible.

CONTENTS

FOREWORD

Growing up I was always told by my parents that "All great things start in Brooklyn," and so, forty years ago when Megan decided to make her early and dramatic entrance (almost in front of a classroom filled with high school students) into the world, I thought I knew what was ahead. I envisioned teacher, lawyer, or even nurse. However, from first grade through our move across the Hudson River, Megan was always the girl organizing events and helping everyone put their best foot forward. Who knew you could have a career, and a great wardrobe, by doing lunch?

Megan has always turned not-so-perfect situations into examples of shining success, so entrepreneurship was simply the natural progression from surviving an unwieldy partnership to founding her own company.

People say daughters are what their mothers make them, but in this case Megan is her own invention!

MARIA DRISCOLL,
Office manager at EvolveMKD and Megan's mom

#MUTUAL ATTRACTION

Doctor, lawyer, teacher, plumber, firefighter, mechanic, soldier, astronaut, athlete, actor, musician, dancer, scientist—the world is full of occupations that are easily understood and easily emulated.

I know a very smart woman who became a dentist simply because she had gone to dentists her whole life and was therefore familiar with what the profession entailed. There was no overriding passion to give the world more perfect smiles. There was no driving force to save every tooth. She just knew what a dentist did and that she could do it too. How she chose her profession is probably pretty much how most people choose. They either have known someone who had a particular job—often a family member—or choose a high-profile career that everyone knows about.

I didn't grow up wanting to own a public relations firm. In fact, I don't know anyone at all who grew up wanting to work in public relations—much less own a firm—because it's not an industry most people know about. When I told my father that I was going to accept an offer in public relations, he was totally bemused. "What are you going to be doing? Planning parties?" No, Dad, it's not planning parties. Well, not all the time.

Why more people don't know about this wonderful way to make a living puzzles me. But then I remember: if I hadn't randomly fallen into the PR world, I wouldn't be running my own business and supporting listed and unlisted companies as well as emerging entrepreneurs that are making a real difference in the real lives of real people.

I can pretty much pinpoint the exact moment I realized that public relations was what I was meant to do.

I was standing in a softly lit room full of people from all walks of life, spanning ages from childhood to "the long-lived elderly"—some clothed, some not. I was holding a glass of champagne and watching my client being swarmed by industry reporters, influencers, and practitioners, all under the watchful eyes of that motley group of onlookers. I looked at this surreal scene and knew I wouldn't want to be anywhere else. This is what public relations was meant to be: a blending of real and surreal, of planned and unplanned, of clothed and unclothed. In my world, public relations focuses on building an attention-getting package around a life-changing product.

The reason no one grows up wanting to be a public relations professional is that if we're doing it right, no one realizes we're there. You never see the legs kicking furiously below the surface. You only see the results—the awesome event that makes everyone talk about the sponsor, the incisive interview that puts the speaker's name on the tip of everyone's tongue, the name of an emerging firm that is suddenly everywhere. Products and entrepreneurs don't just randomly end up on *The Dr. Oz Show* or featured in *People* or contacted to give opinions on recent changes in their industry. They are in that position because an entire corps of public relations professionals made it happen. And believe me, it's not easy. But, it's definitely fun!

It's also unbelievably rewarding. Much like the plumber who never has time to fix the leaky faucets in their own house or the cobbler whose children are barefoot, the field of public relations could do a much better job of promoting itself. In fact, many people who think they understand PR view it as a bit manipulative if not outright unsavory. PR professionals are sometimes thought of as "spin doctors"—which is not meant as a term of respect or endearment.

This perception reminds me of the movies that claim to be "based on a true story." There are bits and pieces of truth in those films, but they are mostly good fiction. The "spin doctor" version of public relations is similar. There are elements of truth (and a few unsavory firms exist out there), but the reality, for the most part, is very different.

The work I do, for example, gets new and often life-changing, life-improving, and sometimes even lifesaving products in front of people who would not otherwise know they exist. I help the entrepreneur with a dream make that dream a reality.

> *I help the entrepreneur with a dream make that dream a reality.*

So, like for most high school grads, public relations was not on my radar as I entered college and began to look ahead to what I would do in life. In fact, I started out on a path that was about as far away from a public relations career as it could be. Instead of studying communications or writing or marketing, I spent my college days as a public policy major at the University of Chicago (U of C), which is the Michael Jordan of economics research and thought. More professors associated with U of C have been awarded the Nobel Prize in Economics than any other institution. This, however, had nothing to do with my decision to attend. My goal was simply to go to the best school possible, and I chose my major from a list of what was available. Public policy, with its good mix of diverse topics, sounded more interesting than any of the others. Economics is pretty much studying what is happening, trying to describe it, and postulating why. Public policy looks for processes and strategies to make people's lives better and works to find ways to balance competing needs. That sounded much more in line with my interests, because it involves creative solutions rather than creative descriptions. (A harbinger of things to come!)

So, what do you do when you are getting ready to graduate from the U of C with a degree in public policy? You begin interviewing for finance jobs. It's pretty much just accepted that U of C graduates become investment bankers, lawyers, or consultants. That's what my parents expected out of their $200,000 investment in my education, and it's what I assumed I would do. Unfortunately, the economy nosedived during the fall of my senior year, so the investment banks that had previously scooped up every U of C grad they could find weren't hiring in the same way. Instead of having a full-time job lined up by October or November of my senior year the way most students before me did, I was still looking for a position well after the holidays.

Although at the time it was nerve-racking to have my graduation date in sight without a job in hand, the situation turned out to be a blessing in disguise. It made me stop and think about what I really wanted to do. And I realized it wasn't finance. That industry didn't energize or excite me. I remember thinking, "They're all wearing pantyhose, and that's just so not me." I was forced to be true to myself—to my fashion sense and otherwise.

I began networking with a lot of my old internship bosses, and one of them thought I'd be good at public relations. My response: "What's public relations?"

It turns out she was right. Much to my father's chagrin, upon graduation I was offered and accepted an internship with the health-care division of a major public relations firm—despite having had to google "press release format" during the skills test—rather than the anticipated full-time financial analyst position offered by a prestigious finance firm. And I never looked back.

The primary thing about public relations that keeps me hooked is its ability to tap into both sides of my personality: the logical, analytical side that aced its way through economics and finance classes and the creative, irreverent side that looks at a challenge and sees a slightly askew solution. It's a niche where being a nonlinear thinker, an analytic problem-solver, and maybe above all a critical listener pays off. It's a career that combines beauty and strength (though I can argue that strength is beautiful in and of itself), art and spreadsheets, and web clicks and return on investment (ROI). It's a constant balancing act between glitz and sensibility.

But best of all, it makes a real difference in people's lives. I recently received a professional achievement award given to U of C alumni "whose achievements in their vocational fields have brought distinction to themselves, credit to the University, and real benefit to their communities." I was on the same stage as the fellow who negotiated NAFTA on behalf of Mexico and a geneticist who is finding cures for orphan diseases (who happened to be the only other woman on stage). I'm sure they thought I was there to hand out the awards rather than receive one. But helping firms that employ hundreds of people succeed, helping medical practitioners provide better products to their patients, helping your everyday consumer learn about products that make them feel better—all this changes lives for the better. And a life changed for the better is always a good thing, whether it is done via a Nobel Prize–winning economic theory or a buzzworthy public relations and social media campaign.

I mention for a reason that the geneticist was a woman and that she and I were in the minority of recipients. When I started EvolveMKD, I wanted to provide high-level jobs and a creative working environment for talented, driven women. Of course, I would hire a qualified man if he was the best fit (and we have wonderful men on staff currently), but when I started, I wanted to provide a space where high-achieving women in particular could thrive. I am proud that EvolveMKD has created more than twenty-five jobs—for both men and women—in the past four years. Only 20 percent of US small businesses have created jobs for others (i.e., have employees)—the vast majority of small businesses are sole proprietorships or partnerships—and out of that group, only 5 percent have created more than ten jobs, according to US Census Bureau data.[1]

I also wanted to focus on representing companies that have a positive impact on consumers' lives. There should be more to working than the bottom line (although I fully recognize that without a positive bottom line, your activities become a hobby rather than a career). But I need to know the work I am doing is going to positively affect others. I have found that the companies having the most positive impact often have a technological, scientific, medical, or engineering bent. In fact, I believe that science-based innovation is the future of healthcare, aesthetics, and lifestyle advances. I wanted my company to be part of that movement.

Traditionally, doctors, scientists, and innovators have neither reached out directly to consumers nor focused on protecting their reputation. With the proliferation of review sites online and the fact that everyone checks these sites before choosing a service provider, it

---

1   "Frequently Asked Questions About Small Business," US Small Business Administration Office of Advocacy (August 2017).

is more important than ever that innovators and firms manage how they are being perceived online. They also need skilled public relations professionals to bring the innovations, medical practices, devices, and so on to the consumer. These companies can't have a positive impact if no one knows about them.

I founded EvolveMKD to fill this gap in the public relations market. The intersection of science and beauty is a niche sector without a lot of competition, because few public relations and social media firms can offer the technical understanding paired with creative execution that EvolveMKD can. We're a company founded on determination, relationships, agility, and sound strategy coupled with a creative spirit.

I have been lucky to be part of the public relations industry during what I think we will look back on as its golden age. During the past fifteen years, the industry has evolved from a narrow definition—which saw public relations professionals being relegated to distributing press releases—to a broader definition, where we are an integral part of planning an overall, omnichannel strategy.

I still remember when I got my first placement on CNN.com. My boss was unimpressed. "No one cares about the dot-com. They want to be on the CNN network." Today, it could not be more different. Public relations is not just press releases and media placement. It's a 360-degree campaign that involves traditional media along with digital space, influencers, personalities, events, social media, videos, and every other way people communicate. It's knowing your target market and how to reach it via the right channel.

On its surface, technology should make our job easier. Instead of calling editors and talk shows individually, we can now reach hundreds of thousands—even millions—of people with the click of a button. But this ease of reach has also changed how media is consumed. We used to talk about broadcasting—NBC, CBS, ABC, and so on—but now it's narrowcasting. During the broadcast days, news was generated and disseminated by a very small group of channels to a broad, heterogeneous audience. Now, everyone can make their own news and have their own channels, which are often limited to those who subscribe. You no longer have pop culture events that everyone is involved in. People now consume media that is focused on their specific interests. Understanding the various platforms, accessing the appropriate niches, and creating targeted content for each one makes our job harder but also makes us more valuable. Because things are changing so much and so quickly, we have to be able to adapt, do a lot of different things, and do them all really well.

The greatest threat to our industry is the lack of understanding from clients on what our job is, what's not our job, what could be our job, and what falls in a gray area. I think public relations is like a mythical unicorn to some people.

And that's why I decided to write this book. I want to help consumers understand how public relations works to bring make-a-difference products to them. And I want to help the developers of these make-a-difference products understand how public relations can raise the awareness of what they are doing.

Remember that wildly diverse group of onlookers in various stages of undress at the event I mentioned earlier? They were all part of *Human Interest: Portraits from the Whitney's Collection* at the Whitney Museum, where we held a private cocktail party to introduce an industry-changing medical device. Surrounding ourselves with portraits depicting people of all ages, of all income levels, and of all walks of life provided the background to drive home the point that this device wasn't just for movie stars or the vain. It could impact the lives of the everyday person as well, because now a procedure that had required invasive surgery could be done noninvasively. That's a huge step in expanding the availability and affordability of any medical process. It's helping people make connections between a highly clinical device, such as this innovation, and its impact on lives that makes my job so rewarding.

In addition, I want to use the story of how EvolveMKD was founded and how it has grown to let others know what I've learned along the way. I knew when I founded the company that there would be challenges—I just wasn't aware of what they were. I was taken by surprise by several that seemed to come out of left field. A couple of times I almost gave up, but I found creative and successful ways to plow ahead and come out on top. I'm sure more challenges will arise as we continue to innovate, but today EvolveMKD is a thriving, growing enterprise that is surpassing revenue and personal goals sooner than I ever would have dreamed.

So, come along with me as I bring you into my world of public relations, social media, and entrepreneurship, where you will find unicorns munching on spreadsheets and bottles of glitter on the same shelf as business-expense receipts. How can you resist?

CHAPTER 1

IN THE #BEGINNING

remember lying in bed and thinking, "This isn't working." And it wasn't just that little voice in my own head that I was hearing. My husband was telling me it wasn't working. My family was telling me it wasn't working. My friends were telling me it wasn't working. If I'd had a dog and she could talk, I'm sure she would have told me that it wasn't working.

I have always prided myself on finding solutions to tough problems and just keeping on until I can find a way to get from here to there. In fact, it was a joke in my family that every year in school I won the Most Improved Player award for whatever sport I was participating in. I don't quit—I find a way to move forward. Yet here I was, almost paralyzed to the point of inaction because a position I'd taken with a mentor less than a year earlier had turned out to be so wrong. Quitting wasn't an option. But neither was continuing as things stood.

I had started the partnership with such high hopes. Moving from an employee to a partner in a privately owned firm seemed like the next logical step in my career. I had worked for the founding partner and thought I knew what I was in for. I expected to be in this partnership for a long, long time. And now I was ready to bail after just a few months. Unthinkable. Totally out-of-character behavior. My MO is to put aside emotion and logically attack the problems until everything is smoothed out. It isn't to cut and run. But here I was, ready to throw my hands up and leave it all.

And that's when EvolveMKD was born—or at least conceived. It would be nearly another year until I was ready to launch, but I was making a plan.

It's also when I really accepted something I've always known intellectually but rarely accepted: not every work problem is fixable. Often, simply moving on is the only fix available. That was certainly the case in this scenario. I thought I knew my partner. But just as you never know what goes on behind closed doors in a marriage, you never know how a company is truly managed until you are part of that management. Our goals were so different. What we thought was important was so different. How we approached life was so different. What we thought made a good partnership was so different. It wasn't just a matter of accepting that there are lots of valid ways to get to the same end point. Our core values simply didn't mesh, and nothing can fix that kind of mismatch.

One of my clients early in my career was a division of a large multinational that had come under fire from people who claimed it was price gouging and engaging in other questionable business practices. If you believed everything you read, it was truly a very bad, no-good actor. However, the firm had brought on new management, including a new CEO and a more transparent and forward-looking board. It had changed its eyebrow-raising ways and would be considered a good corporate citizen with innovative products in anyone's book. But the name still raised questions in the minds of many of its potential investors and customers. The solution we came up with: change the name of the company. Start fresh, and do things the right way.

Starting fresh and doing things the right way is what I did when I founded EvolveMKD.

CHALLENGE **ACCEPTED**

Client: Major beauty brand.

Challenge: Launch new product line.

What EvolveMKD did: Created a "choose your own adventure" format at an Upper East Side townhouse, where the 90 attendees got to discover for themselves the groundbreaking product innovations. Each room at the townhouse was designed to replicate the key benefits and unique ingredients of each product.

Result: Instant social media buzz, a Cosmetic Executive Women (CEW) story recapping the editor's experience, and a *Vogue* exclusive.

LAYING THE FOUNDATION

After thirteen years of working in corporate and agency public relations, I was ready for a career change—not the career itself but in how I was pursuing it. I probably had been for quite some time but didn't know it. I like to say that the universe gives me a signal when it wants me to do something—and being part of an untenable partnership sure looked like an unmistakable signal that it was time to do something entirely different.

I no longer wanted to work for or with any partners, where I had to conform to their standards and compromise my own. I was ready to do public relations the way it should be done. I'd seen the scrappy nature of the smaller firms as well as the strategic (albeit slow-moving) cultures of the big agencies and realized that opportunity existed for an agency offering the best of both worlds for both employees and clients. As far as I knew, no agency was offering the senior-level, hands-on, personalized attention in the healthcare, medical, and beauty spaces that I knew I could provide. Nor was there one that was owned, managed, and predominantly staffed by senior-level women—being a woman-owned agency run by highly skilled women professionals was important to me. The public relations business was changing quickly, not only in the services being offered but in how they were being offered. I wanted to be part of that change by building a public relations and social media agency based on a new model, one where all employees felt they were an integral part of the success and took ownership in its growth.

I also wanted to change the dynamic between the firm and its clients. In a lot of cases, clients view the public relations agency simply as a means to complete a checklist of tasks. They don't appreciate the skill and creativity needed to develop an attention-grabbing campaign with measurable results. I wanted clients who view their agency as an equal partner involved from the beginning in planning strategy all the way through execution to final analysis. I wanted to be free to accept or reject clients based on how they treated us. Making decisions that make others uncomfortable is often hard for women. We are trained from early childhood to be nice. But I knew I could be nice, or at least cordial, and still refuse to work with firms that don't respect my expertise or view me as an equal partner in planning a campaign. You wouldn't think that would be an unusual concept, but in the public relations and social media business, it is.

I've always been a little bit different in how I've approached public relations—more cerebral, logical, and analytical than most others in the industry—and I wanted my firm to reflect those differences. Besides the characteristics I've noted, I had one more major goal: I wanted my firm to prove that public relations is a credible, fact-based industry. A lot of public relations and social media professionals and their clients view the business as a bit squishy. They can see the concrete manifestations—press releases, interviews, mentions in periodicals, an uptick in website clicks—but they don't know how to measure results. They don't know how to analyze all the data that is being thrown at them.

> *I wanted my firm to prove that public relations is a credible, fact-based industry.*

I'm all about measuring results. My college years taught me how to analyze, question, and listen to what the data is really telling me. We should not be doing something if it's not promoting a positive outcome. But how do we know it's positive if we don't have some sort of objective metric to compare it to? I wanted my business to be known for creative solutions, but I also wanted it to be known for its use of data and analytics to confirm that all of that creativity was effective.

The client I mentioned earlier, the one that needed to have its reputation rehabilitated, is the perfect example of some of the features I want to see become standard in the public relations industry. I want to help my clients really understand what they need to do to succeed, and I think there are three main bullet points to that end:

- First of all, if we're dealing with reputation, there has to be real substance behind a company's product or change of heart. Public relations should not be about shading the truth or covering for deficiencies. I drill into our clients that we work only with firms that are not just *saying* the right things but are *doing* the right things and producing real innovation.

- Second, you need to know your audience as well as when to raise media awareness and when to hold back. For the client with the name change, we focused on trade events and media. The plan was to first rebuild the industry's trust in the firm. After that, we would begin to look at a bigger, national rollout. It's a baby-steps approach. We didn't want to blow our whole story without having proof of the changes and products it was built on.

- Third, you must know when not to go out. There are certainly times when it behooves people not to comment or not to get involved in a quarrel. Knowing when to say nothing is as important as knowing what to say. Keeping people out of things when becoming involved would serve no positive purpose is a less appreciated part of what we do, but it is very important, especially when there is crisis.

Finally, I wanted to be able to have a boutique feel but still provide a high level of strategy as well as have traditional public relations and a social media component coexisting under the same roof. Most other agencies the size of mine don't have the right skills in digital and social media, or they don't think it's a priority, or they just focus on traditional public relations methods and channels. Long term, that's not going to be a smart strategy. The smarter strategy, if you can get it to work from a profit and loss perspective, which we have, is to combine traditional media with social media. That's a better offering for clients. We want to provide the senior-level support and access that comes with a smaller-company vibe, which makes clients feel they are really important to the agency, but also offer both traditional public relations along with a digital and social media component. These different branches of public relations need to work very closely together to get the best results.

THE BUSINESS OF BUSINESS

I might have had a good idea of what I wanted EvolveMKD to do, but it turned out I had very little idea how to launch a company that could do it. Looking back to those early days and comparing where I was then to where I am now, I want to shout, "Where's my MIP award?"

When my mismatched partner and I dissolved our partnership, three clients came with me. This was both humbling and a godsend. I was grateful that they had enough confidence in me personally to believe I could provide the service they needed with much less support than I'd had in the past. And I was grateful that I could start EvolveMKD with cash flow from the get-go. Nothing sinks new business ventures faster than a lack of capital. In fact, a lack of capital and negative cash flow is often cited as the number-one reason new ventures fail. Trying to grow revenues while controlling expenses becomes a vicious circle. You need clients to provide a foundation for the company and underwrite services. But you can't get those clients until they are confident that the company is stable and that you can provide the service they need. So, you put in money you don't have with the expectation that you'll attract more clients. If you don't attract them fast enough, your new company will become among the 50 percent that fail in the first five years.[2]

Entrepreneurs tend to focus on developing their product and working with clients when they first start out, but it is the management of your business that can make or break it. The back office needs to be strong and efficient to allow you to do the creative work that will be the hallmark of your firm. It's boring the way the foundation of your house is boring. When things are going well, you don't think about it. When the earth begins to shake, however, nothing is more

---

2   "Frequently Asked Questions About Small Business," US Small Business Administration Office of Advocacy (August 2017).

important than that strong foundation.

There is so much to understand when it comes to business financials. I had no idea how much taxes—hidden and otherwise—fees, and other government-required levies would cut into the cash flow. A good accountant is worth their weight in gold. In fact, a top-notch back-office team can sometimes mean the difference between retaining a client and losing one. We ended up with a client whose previous agency had lost its celebrity endorser because the agency's back office had dropped the ball in paying and following through on contract requirements. When you manage to get a great endorser, you don't want to lose them simply because someone in the office doesn't follow through.

In those first few months of EvolveMKD, when I was working from my kitchen table, I wasn't envisioning employing a team of analysts and finance people. But having the right team to ensure forecasting, hiring, taxation, regulatory compliance, and other management duties are organized and correct is crucial to the success of any business. The data and information your back-office team generates will give you the power to make better decisions and to walk away from things that are not working before they become expensive mistakes.

All management functions are important, but some are more important than others. As mentioned earlier, understanding and managing your cash flow is possibly the most important aspect of business management. Businesses rise and fall on their ability to manage their accounts receivables and payables. Having awareness of this when you are negotiating contracts and understanding the typical pattern of client payments will allow you to make more strategic payment decisions. You always want to be proactive rather than reactive.

THINGS THAT SURPRISED ME

I knew that starting a business would entail some skills I personally didn't have. Accounting and finance activities, for sure. Legal work around contracts and hiring practices, of course. Human relations knowledge of benefits and best practices—I'm all ears. None of this fazed me, however, because I knew I could hire the right people to fill those roles—though hiring the right back-office people turned out to be a challenge in itself.

But in addition to these standard business concerns, I was hit by some roadblocks that I did not expect and that were not so easily navigated.

First of all, I was surprised at how much of an obstacle government can be. I have always looked at government as a force for good. It's there to help. And I still believe this in the abstract. Before government regulations, our land, air, and water were polluted; schools and businesses were segregated; children were working in sweatshops; and women could be fired for being pregnant or even getting married—if they had been hired at all. Overall, government regulations have resulted in a fairer business environment. But the devil is in the details. Government regulations paint with a broad brush held by representatives with little experience in the industries they are regulating. Requirements that might make sense for large companies (which can afford expensive lobbyists in Washington!) or firms in particularly troublesome industries are applied to all, making it difficult and expensive for small businesses to thrive. Government-backed small business loans, the lifeblood of many small businesses, come with a set of requirements and qualifications that are often unrealistic for a small, intellectual-based enterprise. I've learned as a business owner—and this is unfortunately becoming more and more true—that the norm in business is that government isn't really there to help. Sometimes

I wonder if it is purposely trying to be an obstacle. It's something I have to manage for and around. And I'm a female business owner, so I can only imagine what others who have zero programs to help them have to deal with.

I was also surprised by how crucial having professional legal and accounting advice was. I was very fortunate because I had the commitment of three clients before the ink dried on my LLC incorporation documents, so I had revenue from the beginning. That meant I was able to afford a real attorney, a real accountant, and expert advice, all of which went a long way to keeping me out of trouble. I don't think a lot of business owners, especially in the under-forty age group, have the money for that expertise. But hiring professionals is not a luxury. Without them, business owners can end up spending a lot more money than they expected, and they can get their businesses in more trouble without knowing the rules.

I was really surprised at just how hard everything is. For example, I didn't have any idea how difficult finding office space would be. When EvolveMKD outgrew my kitchen table, I thought it would be relatively easy to find several acceptable spaces. EvolveMKD had been profitable from the beginning, and I had pristine personal credit. How wrong I was. No one wanted to rent to me because I didn't have a certain number of years in business. Banks had lending criteria that also relied on how long I'd been in business rather than my profitability. They're just not interested until you pass this magic number of two or three years. I didn't even qualify for a Small Business Administration loan because I wasn't big enough.

I eventually got office space, but even the successes didn't come surprise-free. I was astonished that women are still treated differently than men when it comes to negotiations. It seems to be assumed that I won't negotiate or will give in quickly if I do. And the lawyer for one of the landlords wanted my husband to cosign the lease, even though he has nothing to do with EvolveMKD. That definitely surprised me.

I used to think that people who opened their own businesses were nuts, and now I sometimes think it's people like me, who decide to stay in business, that are kind of nuts. When you're starting out, you don't know what you don't know, so you jump in blindly. And then you find that instead of creating jobs, with government agencies and banks helping you and being part of your network, it ends up being not that way. It feels like you're always fighting for stuff, that it's us against them. I don't know what I thought going into it, but I didn't expect it to be like that.

CHALLENGE **ACCEPTED**

Client: Medical product company.

Challenge: Develop a digital-first campaign to generate brand awareness for a suite of preconception and prenatal tests.

What EvolveMKD did: Starting with a very small social fan base, formulated compelling content and a sophisticated targeting strategy to cultivate an engaged audience. Content included a mix of brand-related messaging and supplementary content that would draw interest from the target audience. Through strategic ad support, the community engaged with the brand and clicked to the website, helping deliver the overall goal of driving toward the sales funnel.

Result: A total of 17.8 million impressions and over 497,000 targeted engagements generated from April 2016 to October 2017. The social fan base grew from 7,000 to 137,000—a 1,857 percent increase—due to hypertargeted and optimized social media ads. Over 88,000 targeted consumers were driven to the brand's website.

BEYOND NUMBERS

Talking about surprises, I was staggered at how much of the business is driven by numbers. I wanted to do public relations and social media, but to do that, I needed a stable wrapper. And that stable wrapper is made of solid revenues and controlled expenses. Yet despite the importance of having control of your numbers, remember that numbers don't always tell the whole story. Yes, if you don't keep track of your cash flow, the entire business can come crashing down. And you always need to consider the impact on your bottom line when making decisions, but you also need to understand the impact of decisions on your corporate culture. How will moving to a new location affect employee retention? Will taking on a large client affect the work-life balance? Providing the services you launched the company to provide and promoting a culture of balance and respect must have equal footing. Public relations is my passion. Knowing that EvolveMKD is making a difference in the industry as well as in the fortunes of our clients is what keeps me pushing through the business stresses.

CHAPTER 2

AND THEN THERE WERE #MANY

EvolveMKD is an experiment in both client service and employee retention. I've worked for enough agencies and watched how multiple others operate to have formed some very definite opinions on what I think is important when it comes to building a team and then retaining those skilled employees. Building a strong team is crucial—you can't do it all alone—and keeping that team in place once assembled is just as important.

LEAD BY EXAMPLE

We foster a team culture at EvolveMKD. Everyone is expected to work together. While certainly an overused buzzword, I do think there is synergy in putting super-talented individuals together in one room. Their individual energies combine and multiply until you have magic. To prove that I really do value teamwork and that it's not just a trite phrase to me, I work as much as everyone else—likely more. How much the owner is invested in the agency sets the tone for everyone. My team knows that we are all in this together and that I wouldn't ask them to do anything I wouldn't do. I'm accessible and spend most of my day interacting with different constituencies. My team knows that although I own the agency, I view us all as equals when it comes to public relations and social media expertise. That matters to people.

I work as much as everyone else— likely more.

CHALLENGE **ACCEPTED**

Client: Skin care company.

Challenge: Introduce science-based skin care line.

What EvolveMKD did: Hosted an interactive event for plastic surgeons that showcased the science behind the brand. Invited editors to a series of beauty treatments to experience the products. Sponsored events that reached mom bloggers and influencers.

Result: Generated unprecedented results with more than 112 million impressions in the six months surrounding the launch. Client indicated that EvolveMKD generated more media results in six months than its previous agency had secured in three years.

BE KIND—DON'T SUCK

I love coming in to work every day because the people who work at EvolveMKD have all bought in to our performance-based culture of respect and kindness. We don't hire mean people—the few times someone has slipped through the cracks, they've been let go quickly. We respect each other's work as well as each other's time. We show up every day to do and be our best.

One thing I've had to learn, however, is that I can't just assume all people have that ethic of hard work and respect built into their core. When I began hiring my team, it never dawned on me that someone might take advantage of the work flexibility and balance that I encourage. I would never do that; why would anyone else? But, unfortunately, some do. So, I've learned that even in a climate of respect, there have to be rules. Wanting to be treated like an adult means you have to act like one. If you don't, I will need to be more rigid in my expectations of behavior. It's not fair to the rest of the team if one member isn't pulling their weight. Leading by example and being careful about whom I hire mitigates this business truth, but it doesn't completely eliminate it.

I also make sure that I show my team members just how much I respect them by taking on only those clients that show us the same respect we show them. Every other place I've worked has put the client on a pedestal. The client is king. Although I definitely think clients should be respected and revered, the relationship needs to be an equal partnership. It's a two-way street. As much as they're choosing us, we're also choosing them. As you get bigger, I think sticking to those values becomes harder, because the stakes get much bigger.

For example, we once had a very large client that had made some substantial changes in management and structure over the years. Some style drift had occurred in what they were trying to accomplish, which made it difficult to develop successful, targeted campaigns. In addition, it seemed we were dealing with a new main contact every few months. And each one contradicted what the previous one had requested. This was turning out to be a terribly unorganized, unpredictable, and unfocused client. Our team was frustrated, because the client was unhappy and let us know it in no uncertain—and sometimes frankly aggressive—terms. On our side, we felt we could never get on the same page because they kept changing the book. If we were deciding whether or not to pitch this client today, we would not pitch them. But they were a huge account for us, and at the time, we were still a small business.

One of the things I had to wrestle with was whether to let the client go because they no longer fit the type of client we engaged with. Or did I keep the client on, because letting them go could mean we'd take a major hit to our growth? We wouldn't have to lay off staff, but it would impact our ability to add anyone new. If I just looked at the numbers, this wasn't even a discussion. I needed to keep the client. But the other data points the numbers don't show you is impact on your culture and impact on your employees. So, even if there's a short-term loss to letting something go, but in the long term I keep my staff consistent and keep everyone happy, then that's the right decision, right? But how much impact would the loss of that revenue have on our ability to do what we wanted to do with the company?

I'm committed to continuing to be discerning as to what types of people we hire and the clients we take on, because I think that makes us different. But I quickly learned that owning a business and being responsible for other people isn't always easy. Decisions have consequences.

LIKE-MINDED PROFESSIONALS

When I hired my first employees, I focused on hiring senior-level staff first. Most agencies hire junior team members first because it's cheaper that way. But I wanted to be able to offer the level of service that our clients could find at the more established agencies—better service, in fact. I also aimed to have a team of complements. I was looking for individuals with specialized talents who would form a well-rounded team. Having a diverse team better positions your business for success in a variety of situations, which is important when you don't yet have a specialist reputation in the industry and are taking on a variety of projects.

Our team members all have public relations and social media experience, but some come from a corporate, in-house environment. Some are from traditional agencies. We also have someone from a nonprofit. So, everyone sees different things, and this results in well-thought-out campaigns that cover a variety of angles.

Conversely, while I looked for a diversity of expertise and backgrounds, I believed I needed to hire people with similar working styles. We were going to be working closely together in a dynamic environment, so our styles needed to mesh. We are all detail oriented and used to a fast-paced environment. People who work at a slow speed wouldn't work well here no matter what their background is, because that's not the speed at which we work.

My hiring strategy has paid off in that every member hired has been able to contribute from the first minute they walked into the office. There was no getting up to speed or learning the ropes. I purposely set out to surround myself with senior-level, like-minded professionals with experience in the field and passion for their work. I did not want to have to manage the people; I wanted to manage the projects.

Although I knew EvolveMKD was going to be a success, it was hard in the beginning to attract the high-level professionals I wanted. If they were super-talented, they already had a very good job. Asking them to give that up and take a risk on my start-up was a hard sell. I will be forever grateful to those who made the jump with me. It got much less hard about a year in. By that time, we had hosted some events. We were becoming known in the industry for our work as well as for our work culture. And with each year, the quality of candidates wanting to work for us has improved. We've recently had many more in-bound applications without proactive outreach by us than we have had in other years.

When I thought about the culture and benefits I wanted to offer my employees, I thought about what I personally would have wanted to receive from an agency. I would have wanted to be treated like an adult and granted a flexible schedule. I would have wanted top-tier health insurance, performance-based bonuses, and a way for my contributions to the overall success of the company to be rewarded. These are the types of things that all employees want, and all companies should be offering them.

The culture at EvolveMKD rewards hard work and allows career advancement opportunities. This involves bonuses, profit sharing, and flexible work schedules. I also encourage professional growth, even if it means team members eventually leave for other opportunities—strong, competent women make the entire industry better.

One of the ways I attract outstanding team members is by offering outstanding benefits. I believe covering health and other insurances as well as retirement plans should just be a standard expense of running a business. In the beginning, I was covering 100 percent of the cost of a top-tier insurance plan. I ended up having to scale back to 70 percent as we grew. The math is very different when you are covering 100 percent of the cost for eight people versus covering at that same level for more than three times that number. We also survey our employees each year to determine if any perks should be added or if some of what I've been offering should be dropped in favor of something else. I want to make sure my employees have choices and that I'm meeting their needs and as many wants as possible. My employees are worth it.

And I think any company that wants to hire and retain the best talent should think about benefits as a prime way to do it.

Finally, I combine this focus on highly skilled hires with a flexible and healthy working environment, which is not a mainstay in the agency world. With few exceptions, the EvolveMKD team is not still in the office at 10:00 p.m. We are home with our families and friends. If I begin to see that work is piling up and the work-life balance is becoming unbalanced, we look for ways to smooth things out. This might mean redistributing work so it can be completed more efficiently. It often means hiring a new team member.

At the same time, I don't want to overhire and then have to take on a client just to pay the overhead. So, it's a constant balancing act. I'm always on the lookout for exceptional people, but I'm also always looking at my numbers. If we met someone amazing whom I couldn't pass on, I would hire them in a heartbeat regardless. Creative companies rise and fall on their talent, and you can't skimp on that. But I've only had

> *Creative companies rise and fall on their talent, and you can't skimp on that.*

that happen once. I made the hire, and we weren't quite sure what she was going to work on, but it all worked itself out because she is so gifted.

But whether we need to find more efficient ways to work or hire a new team member, I always want to find a way to get the team back to a healthy work style. A company can't say it has a set of values and a guiding philosophy and then throw them out the window when things get busy. If a balanced lifestyle is part of your culture, you need to give your employees the ability to achieve that. It makes a real difference in the type of work they will do for you and in their desire to stay with the company.

Using the guiding principles I've outlined above, we've assembled a team that produced results and revenues from day one and that I hope will remain in place for many days to come. Turnover costs money. It may not be actual cash, but it definitely is expensive when people leave. I never wanted people to leave my business because the benefits weren't as good as somewhere else or because the culture was toxic. If people left, I wanted it to be about furthering their career, not because the benefits were better somewhere else.

CHALLENGE **ACCEPTED**

Client: Skin care company.

Challenge: Introduce celebrity model endorser to encourage women to ask their dermatologists for the product.

What EvolveMKD did: Kicked off the partnership announcement with an exclusive article in *People* magazine followed by a press release and a post on the celebrity's social media channels. Introduced the celebrity to key customers at two physician events at a American Society for Dermatologic Surgery meeting to generate buzz across the aesthetic health industry. Organized two media days in New York City that included an intimate tea for beauty editors and a large cocktail party at the trendy Gold Bar in lower Manhattan, where short-lead editors, freelance writers, and influencers were able to have their pictures taken with the celebrity model and share them on social media.

Result: Within two months of the official announcement, secured 88 original placements, garnering over 500 million media impressions in national outlets. Coordinated exclusive coverage of the partnership with *People* magazine as well as broadcast segments on *The Wendy Williams Show*, *Entertainment Tonight*, and *The Dr. Oz Show*. The brand signed up more than 250 new customers and significantly increased revenue within the first few months of the partnership.

CHOOSE WISELY

We hold an annual senior leadership retreat where we talk about challenges facing the agency and our strategic growth plan as well as check in on values issues, including what kinds of clients we want to have. Irrespective of industry, our core strength is in helping clients that provide a product or service that is truly innovative, best in class, or a true improvement over what exists now. The actual industry they represent is relatively unimportant.

We have also determined that it is important to work with clients that have a budget that matches the scope of work they are requiring of us. You would think this would be a no-brainer requirement, but you'd be surprised at how many clients have unrealistic expectations. We want to take on realistic clients who understand the value we provide. Cutting corners or trying to provide champagne service on a beer budget never ends well. It's often tempting to think you can work it all out, especially when you are a young company and finding new revenues is crucial to survival. But in the end, these clients always cost more, whether in real capital or in time, than they bring in.

I mentioned earlier how important it is to have a team with a cultural fit. Having clients with a cultural fit is also important. I've had to fire three clients because they just weren't working out. I've become better at recognizing which ones not to take on, but when I do make a mistake, I've learned to cut my losses early. The problem with taking on a client that doesn't fit, either because they have unrealistic expectations or they don't want to act as a partner, is that they take up time and resources that could be better spent elsewhere. It's better for the company to recognize from the beginning that no matter how much it needs revenues, some clients will cost more than they are worth. You'll save money in the long run—and probably the short run as well—if you just don't take them on to begin with.

In the same way I mentioned earlier that I focused on hiring like-minded professionals, I now focus on being hired by like-minded clients. I get excited about working with the ones that are more entrepreneurial like us, regardless of size. I feel I connect with those business owners on a different level than I used to. At my old agency, I was known for bringing in the large corporate clients—and I still do that—but it's not as much fun as it used to be. Now I really like talking to the owners and dealing with companies that really have interesting technology.

PEOPLE CAN BE SURPRISING

Just as I was surprised by some of the roadblocks I ran into when I was setting up the company, I've found myself surprised by some of the things that have come up when managing a team. I had considered myself a pretty savvy manager, but being the owner is an entirely different ball game. I'm a straight shooter, a what-you-see-is-what-you-get type of person, and I tend to think other people are just like me. But they're not. Managing employees, not just a staff, has come with a set of its own surprises.

Primarily, I didn't realize how much the responsibility of having people rely on me for their livelihood would weigh on me. I've managed people before, but it's a different feeling when you're responsible for everyone's jobs. It's so awesome in one respect, but it's also a huge responsibility. You're integral to people's lives. You're providing their income and their health insurance. Every decision on accepting a client or not, on adding staff or not, on spending revenue for one thing or another comes with an overlay of how this will affect the bottom line and other people's lives. I was surprised about what that felt like and how much energy that really takes.

And I was also surprised by how some employees sometimes take advantage of the system, because that's just not part of my DNA. I work with an amazing group of people. I've been very lucky the vast majority of the time. But it surprised me that I had to set up boundaries and processes for adults, because a very few might feel it is okay to be less than 100 percent ethical all the time. That was very surprising.

What didn't surprise me is how much I love what I'm doing. I love the people. I love the work. And truth be told, I love the competition. I love the adrenaline rush of signing a new client, of reaching a revenue goal, of being asked to appear on a TV talk show. I don't think any entrepreneur can succeed if they aren't all in.

And I want you to be all in. Stay with me while I now take you through what really sets EvolveMKD apart and how I believe we can change the industry for the better.

CHAPTER 3

DEEP-DIVE #ANALYTICS SPRINKLED WITH WHIMSY

A s I turned out the lights at the end of a recent event, I felt as if I should be sprawled in a high-backed chair while wearing torn fishnet stockings and a slightly askew feather boa with a word bubble over my head saying, "Wow! That was good!" A handheld fan and short bedazzled dress would complete the picture.

This was a particularly well-attended event, and I was thoroughly spent but energized at the same time. I've felt the same way when making a basket against a crosstown rival after dribbling the entire court. Waves of thunder hit me as the home crowd roars its approval. I throw my arms in the air in jubilation! Then I collapse on the bench to catch my breath.

Although the sense of euphoria after a great basket and a well-attended public relations event is similar, the definition of success couldn't be more different. A successful basketball shot is obvious—the ball goes through the hoop. A successful public relations or social media event is a bit more nuanced. When we host a campaign event, we are first of all looking for bodies through the door. But that is just the baseline. We need those bodies to translate into increased visibility for our client. Counting the attendees is easy. Objectively determining the positive outcome for our client is harder.

CHALLENGE **ACCEPTED**

Client: Cutting-edge CBD company.

Challenge: Break into mainstream media with a nontraditional product launch.

What EvolveMKD did:

- Capitalized on national holidays, such as Earth Day and 4/20, as well as cannabidiol as the latest trending beauty ingredient, resulting in media coverage in *Health, Marie Claire,* ELLE.com, Allure.com, TODAY.com, Total Beauty, TheCut.com, and more.
- Aligned the brand with fitness influencers to demonstrate the pain management benefits of CBD, resulting in numerous organic social media mentions and a media and influencer event highlighting the company's products.
- Connected the brand with new retail opportunities through physician relations, including product sales at dermatologist and chiropractor practices.
- Organized ongoing customized product send-outs and one-on-one meetings across beauty, fitness, and lifestyle media and influencers as well as identifying product sampling opportunities to get priority products directly into the hands of the target consumer.

Result: Nearly five hundred million media impressions and over three million social media impressions in first year of launch. In addition, more than 50 national media and influencer attendees were at the launch event. Organic product mentions on more than 100 influencer social media channels, including reality Bravo and E! TV stars, as well as leads for new retail opportunities.

MEASURING THE INVISIBLE

In the past, a typical conversation between a public relations professional and a client often went something like this:

Client: *What are you going to do for me?*

Professional: *We are going to host a media event, we are going to blanket the news outlets with press releases, and we might even put something on a Facebook page.*

Client: *That sounds good. How do you know it will be working?*

Professional: *We'll count the mentions in publications and other media, and we'll look at how many clicks you get on your website.*

Client: *Sounds good to me. Send me a bill.*

That was often as deep as the client wanted to get into the details of a campaign. And frankly, a whole lot more details to get into didn't exist. But over the past few years, companies have rightly become laser focused on their bottom line and getting value for their money. EvolveMKD works primarily with innovators, particularly in the medical, beauty, and pharmaceutical fields. These are not the high-flying dot-com start-ups of the 1980s and 1990s, which were often better known for their marble-floored offices and foosball tables than their products. Today's innovators are extremely savvy businessmen and women who have a life-changing product or service and know they need help getting the word out to their target market.

A typical conversation with this sort of client might go something like this:

Client: *What are you going to do for me?*

Professional: *We are going to look at the people you want to reach and make sure we use multiple channels to reach them.*

We'll hold a press event to introduce you to the media. We'll make sure reporters, writers, influencers, and others receive information on your product and what makes it new. We'll help the media understand why it is so innovative. We'll position you as an expert by getting you on panels and making sure you are the go-to person when any media outlet wants a comment or information about your niche. We'll look at a celebrity, key opinion leader, or other well-known personality—in other words, an influencer—to put a familiar face to what might be seen as an esoteric concept. And we'll protect your reputation. We'll enhance your stature in the industry while guarding against any negative media chatter. We'll use traditional outlets as well as social media and other digital formats. We'll give you a 360-degree campaign.

Client: *That sounds good. How do you know it will be working?*

Professional: *We'll count the mentions in publications and other media, and we'll look at how many clicks you get on your website. That will tell us that people are seeing your name. We'll also, of course, look at the business results you are getting during the time period the campaign is running.*

Client: *Okay. But what does that mean to me? How does that translate into action and measurable results?*

And this is where the rubber meets the road in public relations. Marketing, advertising, and public relations often get mixed together in a client's mind. We are distinct food groups, though I admit the boundaries can get more than a bit blurred. We all work together for one purpose, and clients sometimes wonder why they need all three. Couldn't they get along with just marketing and advertising and save a little money and a lot of time in the process?

In an earlier chapter, I mentioned that I wanted to start an agency that did public relations the way I thought it should be done. Part of that is having a firm where traditional media and social media, traditional public relations and digital publications, can all reside under one roof. Part of that is leading a team of like-minded professionals who take their roles seriously—personally, even. Part of it is being seen as a strategic creative partner by the client and not just a group to execute predetermined tasks. And part of that is having a firm known for its outstanding, measurable results.

Focusing on objectively measurable results and how they are driving audience interaction isn't typical for the industry, but it should be.

Focusing on objectively measurable results and how they are driving audience interaction isn't typical for the industry, but it should be.

The roadblock to measuring the success of a public relations and/ or social media campaign is that we have no single, objectively vetted metric that tells us we have succeeded. I'm all about data. I want to be able to look at a spreadsheet of numbers and say, "This worked—you can see it in these numbers," or conversely, "This didn't work—look at these numbers."

I also want to be able to pinpoint the "why." I might see from the numbers that web traffic obviously spiked, but what part of the campaign drove that spike? What was it that not only grabbed attention but created a call to action?

If we were selling something tangible, it would be easier to determine if our activity were resulting in more sales. We'd count the number of llamas sold before our campaign and compare that total to the number of llamas sold after the campaign. Improving awareness of a product or polishing the reputation of a client is harder to measure. But that doesn't mean we don't try.

Having a consistent way to track our progress is so important that EvolveMKD commissioned the primary author of the Barcelona Principles to help develop our firm's measurement and evaluation program. The Barcelona Principles is a system of communications measurement used by a wide spectrum of firms, from emerging start-ups to the *Fortune* 50 and from nonprofit to publicly listed companies.

We felt an EvolveMKD version was needed to put things into our own language while staying true to the original theory and intent.

The resulting EvolveMKD Principles of Measurement are the basis of how we approach communications measurement and evaluation. This system can not only objectively track results but allows us to set realistic goals in the first place and then explain to our clients what we are doing. This concept might not seem revolutionary to people in other fields, but it is relatively rare in the public relations industry.

THE EVOLVEMKD DIFFERENCE

The thing that makes the EvolveMKD measurement system different—and we believe stronger—than other systems is that we have shifted the focus from input and activity measurement to outcome and impact evaluation. A fisherman who catches twenty fish might have nothing to show for it if none of them were keepers. We want to track those keepers, not just absolute numbers.

The EvolveMKD system was more than a year in the making, so it is a very robust system. But on the surface, it is relatively simple. Briefly, we begin by sitting down with the client to define the business or organizational challenge to be solved. We then talk about and agree on the output and outcome definitions that best suit the client's specific opportunity or challenge.

Once the challenge is well defined, we move into a very important part of the discussion: What does successful voice, reach, and engagement look like? What and how does successful awareness, understanding, perception, behavior, and recommendation look like? What's worked in the past, and what hasn't? What information exists now about the shape of the outcome and output funnels, as in conversion rates and time to conversion from each level to the next?

Engaging the client in what success looks like is crucial. It's not unusual for a client to start by saying something like, "We just want more sales." But that's not a public relations goal. That's a sales goal. Good communications measurement goals involve determining the right target audience (who); the outputs, outcomes, and organizational impact (what); a specific number or percent (how much); and a specific date (when).

A full-throated public relations / communications goal might be the following:

- To drive purchase of CBD-based face creams among women aged forty to seventy with a Herfindahl-Hirschman Index (HHI) at least 25 percent higher than the median US HHI, the following measurable outcomes of communications need to happen:

- XXXXXX percent of possible consumers are **aware** of CBD-based face creams (awareness).

- XXXX percent of possible consumers **understand** what CBD-based face creams are (understanding).

- XXX percent of possible consumers **believe** that CBD-based face creams improve beauty economically and better than other such creams (perception).

- XX percent of possible consumers **purchase** CBD-based face creams (behavior).

- X percent of possible consumers **recommend** CBD-based face creams to other possible consumers (recommendation).

Once we have worked together to nail down a set of measurable goals, we look at timing. Some goals can be accomplished within six months while others should become part of a three-year plan. In both cases, we look hard at what is realistic and what resources are needed to get there. One of our company mantras is "Don't build a spaceship if you are only trying to go to the grocery store." In other words, we tailor our services to each client's needs and budget, and we don't engage in overkill.

MEASURING EVERYTHING WE CAN

The foundation of our measurement system isn't entirely new. It's based on things we already measured. But how we are putting those inputs together to provide an interwoven picture that tells a story *is* new. In addition, we aren't just measuring inputs—though we need those inputs. Instead, we are measuring outcomes. How do those inputs impact the product or organization?

Even before our consultants worked with us to develop EvolveM-KD's measurement system, we weren't entirely working blind. We might not have had a perfect data metric, but there were—and are—lots of things we *could* measure to give us an idea of how well we were doing. Because measuring perceptions is squishy, we look for proxies. We look for tangible ways to measure the intangible. One of the go-to metrics for everyone in the industry is "eyeballs" on the material. To get an estimate of the number of people who have come across our clients' products or services, we count the clicks on a website or the mentions in media sources. If there are more this month than last, we declare success. But in reality, this is a pretty crude measure of success. We don't know what those extra clicks tell us. Are those people translating into sales? Or are they just curious lookie-loos? Are they forming better opinions of a product, procedure, or client because of our work? How would we know that?

Saying, "We want to raise awareness—we want more people to know about us," is pretty nebulous. What do you want them to know about you?

Oscar Wilde is credited with saying, "The only thing worse than being talked about is not being talked about." This witticism eventually morphed into the oft-heard declaration "There's no such thing as bad publicity" often attributed to P. T. Barnum, but no one really knows where it came from. Then came its more direct corollary, "All publicity is good publicity."

Apropos to nothing (I just like it), the Irish writer Brendan Behan added his spin to the sentiment by clarifying, "There's no such thing as bad publicity except your own obituary."

P. T. Barnum and other cynics to the contrary, bad publicity is rarely good publicity. Unless you are a reality TV personality or maybe a rapper, bad publicity can derail a career faster than Hamptonites leaving Manhattan on a Friday afternoon in summer. Tiger Woods is a perfect example. As news of his personal behavior hit the wires, he went from being known as the best golfer in the world to being known as the man whose wife chased him down the driveway in the middle of the night while swinging a three iron (or was it a two iron?). Sponsors dropped him like a hot potato. *Business Insider* estimated that he lost $22 million in endorsements from 2009 to 2010.[3] Woods has made strides since then to recoup some of his good-guy image.

---

3   Will Wei, "Tiger Woods Lost $22 Million In Endorsements In 2010," *Business Insider* (July 21, 2010), https://www.businessinsider.com/tiger-woods-lost-22-million-in-2010-endorsements-2010-7

Tabloids carry pictures of him with his children. The Golf Channel runs regular features on how hard he is working to overcome his back (and other) injuries. Fans are pulling for him to make a comeback, and the huge galleries are back to following him on the course. Despite all the positive vibes around him at the moment, however, no one will ever forget his epic fall from grace.

More recently, former PBS host Charlie Rose saw a stellar reputation, built over decades, disappear within minutes—or whatever the length of one news cycle is. I'm sure you can name a multitude of others.

Bad publicity has an outsized impact on a person's or company's ability to operate. No one wants to be associated with a tarnished star because they don't want to be pulled down by the surrounding negative vibes—and there are usually untarnished options to choose from. It is exponentially harder to change a negative impression than to enhance a good one. That means a large part of my job is to guard my clients against bad publicity so they never have to dig themselves out of that hole.

But an even larger part is generating good publicity. I think my team is pretty outstanding at generating newsworthy buzz, but what does that translate into? It's not hard to measure how much we've improved awareness—there are all kinds of surveys and apps that can help us determine the level of awareness before and after a campaign—but is just knowing about a product enough? It's certainly a necessary start, but shouldn't that awareness translate into some sort of positive action? And is there an objective tipping point in the awareness curve where enough people know about the company or product that you can now expect increased sales? If so, what is it?

A little earlier in the chapter, I mentioned that the EvolveMKD measurement system first sets realistic goals (you wouldn't think that would be a noteworthy concept, but it is). After that, we develop a campaign that allows us to measure outputs, outcomes, and organizational impact. We measure "why" as much as "how much." What makes this measurement system different is that we aren't just counting eyeballs or impressions. As noted above, that doesn't tell us exactly how the consumer is perceiving the client or product. Instead, we measure the following:

- **Voice**—How loud was your voice? Building a presence in a particular communications channel. This is a pure quantity measure of how "loud" our voice is versus whether the communications are working.

- **Reach**—Did they hear you? Breaking through the "noise" so people hear you and are reached with your messages.

- **Engagement**—Did they respond to you? Two-way dialogue with stakeholders and/or where someone who has been reached in turn takes some form of action on that content.

When setting goals and measuring outcomes, defining what we mean is important. In our case, we use the following definitions:

- **Awareness/Familiarity**: The percentage of a target audience that has heard of something (e.g., 90 percent of possible consumers have heard of the product or service)

- **Understanding**: The percentage of a target audience that understands something and/or how well the audience understands something (e.g., 70 percent of possible consumers understand what the product or service is)

- **Perception**: The percentage of a target audience that believes something and/or how strongly they hold that belief (e.g., 50 percent of possible consumers think the product or service is worth buying)

- **Behavior**: The percentage of a target audience that does something (e.g., 30 percent of possible consumers buy the product or service)

- **Recommendation**: The percentage of a target audience that recommends something to their friends, families, colleagues, and so on (e.g., 20 percent of possible consumers recommend the product or service to friends, family, and colleagues)

When setting goals, we need to be aware that the percentage will decline with each step from awareness to recommendation. More people need to be aware of something than will understand it than will think it is optimal, and so on. No matter how loud one is (voice), not everyone will hear you (reach). Of those who hear you, not every person engages.

TURNING IMPERFECT METRICS INTO REALLY GOOD METRICS

Our measuring and evaluation system is based on putting objective numbers to concepts that public relations firms have used for years as well as deciding which of those concepts is really telling us what we need to know. For example, if we are just measuring clicks, we are measuring a lot of noise. We want to measure the number of clickers who actually hear our message. Focusing on this "reached" group of consumers would be similar to looking at the "share of mind" concept in marketing.

"Share of mind" is a marketing concept that involves working to make sure your brand is the first one people name when thinking about a specific grouping. It's like using Ferrari as an example of expensive foreign sports cars, Tiffany as an example of high-end jewelry, or Mother Teresa as an example of altruism. It's generally considered the gold standard in branding. But it works both ways.

You can have negative share-of-mind rankings as well. Harvey Weinstein will always be top of mind when talking about sexual harassers; Enron will always rank highly when talking about unethical corporate practices; and it seems unlikely that pharma-bro Martin Shkreli will ever live down his image as the poster child for heartless, money-grubbing CEOs (not least because it's a pretty accurate image).

"Share of voice" (SOV) is the public relations equivalent of share of mind. It's defined as the percentage of coverage and conversations about your brand from all sources—traditional print, traditional media, digital print, and social media—relative to your competitors. Traditionally, we also use "share of impressions" (SOI), which measures the percentage of the total number of people who might have had the opportunity to be exposed to your company's coverage relative to your competitors. For example, if we secure mentions in an article appearing in the United Airlines *Hemispheres* publication, there is the possibility that more than eleven million people will see it though one of the publication's print, mobile, social, or digital channels. We know that realistically, every one of those eleven million travelers won't be reading the magazine, but we are looking at possibilities. You can't have an actuality without first having a possibility.

When SOV and SOI metrics are compared, we can get a good idea of the number of eyeballs on our client. It also gives us an idea of the quality of the media that mentioned our client. For example, if we aren't seeing as many mentions as our competitors are getting (low SOV numbers) but we have a high SOI, it usually means that the outlets that *are* picking up our message have better circulation numbers or a more active follower engagement—and are therefore likely higher quality—than some of the channels mentioning our competitors. We usually want to be in those better-quality publications or on those more widely watched talk shows. This might mean we are actually getting better coverage than a competitor with more mentions, because we are being seen by a higher-quality or better-targeted demographic. But frankly, we don't know that if we don't dig deeply into the numbers to see exactly who is seeing the campaign material.

We certainly want to win the competition for both SOV and SOI, but we want to make sure what is being talked about is positive. With the growth of social media in the past decade, negative stories and perceptions—true or untrue—spread exponentially. The old game of telephone, where children sit in a circle and whisper a phrase in the ear of the next person and then laugh at how wildly the phrase is distorted by the end, has nothing on how quickly rumors can be distorted and spread on social media. Dominating the conversation because your client has become involved in a scandal—real or rumored—is a public relations nightmare.

When you consider how important reputation is to a successful venture, you can understand how seriously I have to take my job. I feel the wins and losses personally, because a loss can cripple a client's future growth while a win can send them on to the next level. And because I take on clients with products and services that truly benefit people, a win for my client is a win for a huge representation of our target audience.

It would be easy to say that success in public relations is simply making sure our clients survive the digital age with their reputations intact while raising awareness of their products, innovations, or services. But I want it to be more. I want to be able to prove that our creative events, awareness-raising activities, and press-exposure processes have a measurable, positive effect. I want to be able to analyze our campaigns with the same precision that salespeople use to analyze their numbers. My time at U of C taught me how important analysis is. You can never be sure that surface perceptions are correct. You need to separate fact from biases and unsubstantiated conclusions.

REPURPOSING TRADITIONAL MEASUREMENT TOOLS

Before I go too far down the road of how we measure and analyze success today and how we would like to measure it in the future, let's start with what success looks like. In broad, nonanalytical terms, success is taking a client from where they are now to where they want or need to be. Finding creative ways to get there is the job of all public relations. Finding creative ways to get there while producing measurable, replicable results is the mission of EvolveMKD. The "measurable, replicable results" are as important as the creative, whimsical, buzzworthy campaigns. Without measurable results, the campaigns are just a good time had by all. That's not a bad goal if you are throwing a dinner event or planning a tailgate party, but it's not what our clients are paying us for. They want—and deserve—to know that they are getting an acceptable ROI.

If you've read this far, you might be thinking that there is no way to measure how successful a public relations or digital media campaign is. That's not quite true. We have lots of ways to measure our activity. We just don't have a perfect way. Much of what we do involves looking at lots of different analytics and then hypothesizing what part public relations had in those outcomes. It's a bit like how scientists talk about black holes. Before the first picture of a black hole hit the airwaves in 2019, no one had actually seen a black hole—we surmised they existed by the activity around them.

To capture the activity that results from a public relations / digital media campaign, we look at it from a variety of angles. Before we begin, we need to determine a baseline for various measurements. What kind of traffic is the website experiencing? How much does our target market already know about the product or procedure? Is it what we want them to know? After we have established the baseline measurements, we move on to pinpointing how our campaigns have improved awareness and positive perceptions.

First of all, we simply look at **how much coverage** the campaign generated. How often was the client mentioned in the traditional press, trade publications, digital outlets, and social media as well as on television and the radio? We then break that raw number down into categories to determine how much of that coverage was extemporaneous—meaning the host or writer mentioned the client without our help—and how much resulted from our placing advertorials, press releases, or other EvolveMKD or customer-generated material. We will generally see mentions increase over the months and quarters as the product or innovator becomes better known and as we develop relationships with reporters and industry insiders. You would like to think that reporters and other writers base their articles on objective metrics, but we are all human. Reporters and feature writers prefer to work with people they like and who they know will respond to requests—just as we all do. The better and stronger the relationships we build, the better the coverage for our clients.

We then look at the **quality of that coverage**. This is where SOV and SOI come into play. We want to dominate any conversation involving our clients' product categories. For example, if a talk show is discussing the merits of gastric bypass, we want to make sure our client's less invasive procedure is talked about and compared favorably to other options. We also want to be seen by the widest number of people possible. SOI tells us how many people are seeing our client's story—mentions in publications with high readership will result in a higher SOI, even if the client doesn't dominate those articles. Achieving high numbers in both SOV and SOI is the ultimate goal. If you aren't scoring well on a SOV index but are rising to the top in the SOI ratings, it usually means you are getting the majority of your coverage from highly read or viewed sources but aren't dominating the conversation. You need to amp up the message to convert that high SOI into a high SOV.

We also look at **tonality of coverage**. Was the coverage positive? Was it negative? Was it only okay? In terms of where the product is mentioned, is it in the headline? Is it in the body? Is it mentioned once? Twice? Is the messaging the company really wants to focus on pulling through? We know we could say a lot of different things about various products, but are our work and our initiatives really allowing the media and consumers—via social media and other outlets—to home in on the topics we want them to home in on?

Although all the coverage metrics are important, the tonality metric is maybe the most important to any public relations / digital media campaign, because making sure the market is hearing the message the client wants to promote is our respon-

> *It doesn't help if the message is dominating the media if the message is wrong.*

sibility. It doesn't help if the message is dominating the media if the message is wrong. In fact, it hurts. I don't know why the human brain holds on to a wrong message so much longer than a right message, but it does. Every time.

A major part of tracking the tonality is keeping watch on how our overall message is playing. We focus on innovators, particularly in the medical, scientific, and beauty fields. For many of our clients, there is an intersection of these three sectors, where science is used to drive innovative beauty and medical products. These innovators want to change the bigger conversation, so we are not just talking about superficial beauty but about how scientific breakthroughs in skin rejuvenation can be incorporated into products. They want to change the conversation from how medical devices hold up under surgical conditions to how innovative procedures and devices make surgery more comfortable and less invasive for the patient while improving overall outcomes. To this end, we track how this message is being received, even if our clients' products or innovations aren't specifically mentioned.

Up until a few years ago, nearly all "counting eyeballs" referred to the number of people who saw your client's name in a written publication or on television. Today, everyone lusts after digital mentions. We, along with nearly everyone else, use Google Analytics to track the growth of traffic to a client's website. Although digital communications is the way the world is moving, and we have no choice but to move with it, we actually like this shift to digital traffic because it is so easy to follow. We can see immediately if there is a spike in website hits after a campaign event or television mention. We can follow how many retweets we get on Twitter or how many shares we get with an article posted online. If we are using blog posts to drive traffic (blogs are really, really hard to execute consistently, so we don't use them as often as some other groups do because we usually need the client to consistently commit to spending time on them as well), we track which ones drive the most traffic and result in the most shares. We also look at which social media sites are driving the most referrals and put more time into those. In fact, we track all traffic and note where it is coming from—a social media campaign, an influencer's endorsement, a TV appearance—and skew the overall plan toward channels that are grabbing the most attention. Analyzing the data allows us to optimize productive approaches and de-emphasize less productive channels to build momentum over time.

Public relations firms are no longer complete if they don't include digital capabilities along with traditional services. The skills needed for the two are different, so we have two different teams under our roof. We no longer are just interested in placing content or having reporters pick up press releases. We want to engage our target market in our clients' products. We want an active community, and we consistently track the engagement and growth of that community. Our focus metric for social media is to measure engagement of consumers by tracking shares, likes, comments, and questions but most importantly conversions. Conversion metrics include things like video views and a website call to action. Conversions are easily measured with pixels and also allow us to build, target, and retarget custom audiences without any third-party sources. (This also helps us guard against bots, which are fake followers and skew the numbers if we allow them to proliferate.) We also look at the demographic breakdown of engaged users and make sure it matches up with the audience we're trying to reach. If it doesn't, we can tweak our campaign to make sure we're attracting the right kind of people to interact with our client's digital channels.

The expansion of digital has opened up new avenues for public relations professionals to get their message to the market. One of the biggest opportunities revolves around video strategy. To engage the audience even more, video content can be hosted on social media channels and supported through hypertargeted social media ads. Longer-format videos can be posted to YouTube and Facebook directly, while shorter-form videos are more optimal for platforms like Instagram and YouTube. Facebook and Instagram also have live-streaming options, which are currently favored by the platforms. With targeted social media ad support driving reach and views, content can be targeted to key audiences.

Social media and digital content channels have been game changers when it comes to tracking awareness. In the good old days, we couldn't do that. We could track how many mentions we had in the media, but we didn't know how prospects were reacting. Unless customers told a salesperson that they had seen the product on a specific TV show or in a specific article, there was no way to track ROI. Digital channels have changed all that.

CHALLENGE **ACCEPTED**

Client: Major skin care company.

Challenge: Generate brand awareness and product buzz across social media through organic placements and strategic paid campaigns with brand-right influencers.

What EvolveMKD did: Partnered with LIKEtoKNOW.it on an influencer affiliate partnership campaign, working with five lifestyle and beauty influencers to specifically lift sales at retail partner Sephora. Aligned the brand with a prominent celebrity makeup artist to drive brand credibility and product efficacy. Scheduled ongoing product send-outs across a targeted community of fashion, lifestyle, and beauty influencers to highlight product usage, benefits, and beauty routine integration.

Result: Over 8.9 million social media impressions. Drove a 50 percent increase in retail partnership sales. Created a thirteen-minute organic video with YouTube beauty superstar Tati Westbrook solely featuring the brand.

IMPACTFUL MEASUREMENTS

With all the different apps and analytics used for measuring, producing data sometimes feels like an end unto itself. It's not. We don't just measure for the sake of measuring. All these numbers get sliced, diced, massaged, and analyzed until we have a clear picture of what is working and, most importantly, why. We need to let our clients know how we are driving leads and increasing traffic to enhance their bottom lines. We need to show them via reports how the public relations campaigns are impacting the organization.

The EvolveMKD measurement system is a huge step in moving the role of public relations out of a touchy-feely world into a fact-based spreadsheet. We have changed the conversation from "How many impressions?" to "What is the target market hearing?" We are focused on the impact of actions, not just the number. No "How good does this feel?" subjective data. We focus on quality over quantity. I'm sure there will be more tweaking of metrics and reports as we implement our system over time and clients, but we feel we are on the right path. (There's that "feel" word again!)

All this talk about analyzing and ranking results leads us to the next chapter, which is focused on what is involved in a typical campaign at EvolveMKD. After all, without the campaign, there would be nothing to analyze.

CHAPTER 4

THE 360-DEGREE #CAMPAIGN

When I started in public relations, it was all about the press release. What kind of headline attracts attention? Should it be hand delivered, emailed, or snail-mailed? What is the best time for it to arrive on the editor's or reporter's desk? We've come a long way since those days.

As outlined in the previous chapter, EvolveMKD has spent a lot of time working on integrating analytics into our campaigns. I personally want to be able to see how well a public relations and social media campaign works, but I also want to be able to provide that data to clients. We want to move them from thinking "A public relations and social media campaign would be nice to have" to "Look at these numbers! A public relations and social media campaign is something we must have."

In the same way that the emphasis on ROI has changed over the years, with clients wanting more proof that their public relations dollars are being used wisely, the type of campaign now needed to be successful has changed.

The public relations model has been slow to change. Since its beginnings, public relations firms and professionals have typically been specialized and stayed within their lanes. You might be a pro at getting press releases and client-generated material placed. Or you might have the type of industry contacts that result in your clients being featured on major industry panels. Or maybe you stage events that every media outlet wants to attend. Rarely, however, do you do everything well. The growth of social media and digital communications has further complicated the industry, as the vast majority of firms do either traditional public relations *or* digital marketing. I want to change that.

In today's fast-paced information world, our clients deserve more than a traditional plan or a digital plan. They need and deserve it all—traditional, nontraditional, digital, and whatever else is available. We like to say we provide a 360-degree campaign for our clients, but in reality, it is more like a 41,253-square-degree campaign. (That's the number of square degrees in a sphere, for you readers who haven't opened a geometry book since high school.) We aren't just surrounding our clients with one-dimensional channels to their right and left, front and back. We are looking at every angle—top, bottom, front, back, side to side, acute, and obtuse. Name the angle, and we are working it.

In the past, it was enough to cultivate relations with reporters and get your press releases into the mainstream and trade publications. If your client was particularly well spoken, you might work to get them onto a panel or even a talk show. Life was pretty straightforward.

Today, that straight-line strategy won't cut it. You need to present your message and your clients across all platforms—traditional and nontraditional, digital and video—and you need to home in on both the brand and the person behind the brand.

CHALLENGE **ACCEPTED**

Client: Beverage purification company.

Challenge: Launch the company's first product to consumers and media via traditional public relations and social media.

What EvolveMKD did: Hosted an interactive event with Bravo's *Top Chef* that featured a customized dinner and wine pairing. Seeded product via unique mailer to influential social media taste-makers to drive product buzz and interest. Developed branded social media content that highlighted brand persona and product benefits. Implemented a robust social media advertising campaign that targeted core audience across multiple digital platforms.

Result: Product sold out in the first month of sales as a result of robust press coverage, including *The Doctors*, the *TODAY* show, and *Food & Wine* magazine. Social media was consistently the top website traffic driver (outside of major media hits) to the brand's website, which was the primary point of purchase.

CREATING A CAMPAIGN

The best way to describe a 360-degree campaign is to follow clients from the time they sign with us through the campaign development to execution and analysis. Because EvolveMKD focuses on innovators who are making a real difference in people's lives—which generally translates into researchers, inventors, and innovators in the beauty, medical, and lifestyle sectors—let's look at the hypothetical Dr. Smythe, an Australian research and development scientist focused on nutrition. Dr. Smythe has developed a nutritional tonic that helps normalize blood chemistry, resulting in lowered cholesterol, controlled blood sugar, and reduced inflammation. In addition, it promotes weight loss. In his native Australia, the tonic is recognized as an option for controlling type 2 diabetes and cholesterol. It has also become the go-to diet aid for those looking to lose more than ten pounds.

Dr. Smythe and the company he works for would now like to bring this product to the US, but they face some formidable hurdles.

First of all, no one in the US has heard of Dr. Smythe or his nutrition-based company. Why would health food stores stock this product (and would that even be the best distribution channel)? Why would a consumer concerned about health or weight choose this product over the multitude of well-known American products already on the shelves?

Secondly, the supplement and diet industry is largely unregulated. As such, it has a well-deserved "buyer beware" reputation. Middle-of-the-night infomercials are full of smiling promoters hawking their products as the answer to all your weight problems. Dr. Smythe is going to have to rise above this chatter and prove that his product actually is effective.

Thirdly, the diet and supplement industry is saturated with products. Consumers are bombarded with product advertisements and promotions all day long. Most have learned to tune them out. Dr. Smythe is going to need to cut through that if he is going to raise awareness of his tonic.

FIRST THINGS FIRST

Before we take on a new client, we always meet with them to determine if we are a good match. I view us as hiring the client as much as the client is hiring us. We need to make sure our values sync up and that everyone agrees on what is realistic, both in budget and results. The budget and expectations are easy to suss out. Value-matching is more difficult. To be successful, we believe we need to be a strategic partner from the beginning. At EvolveMKD, we don't view public relations and digital marketing as simply executing tasks given to us by the client's marketing or advertising team. We want a seat at the table when strategy is being determined, when marketing is being outlined, when advertising is being overlaid. We believe that for a campaign to be successful, it needs to be part of an integrated plan—and we need to be part of developing that plan.

I like to think that marketing is the curb appeal. It brings the prospect in so that the sales agent can make the sale. But the public relations group is the stager. We create a welcoming ambience so that the prospects want to stay and find out more. We raise awareness that the property exists and create the perception that everything connected with the property is something prospects want to be involved with too.

Because we primarily deal with innovators, we also want to make sure their new development or advancement is legitimate. We aren't scientists, but we need to know that the claims being made—and the claims we will be promoting—are sound. We are putting the reputation of EvolveMKD on the line every time we take on a client, and we wouldn't be very good public relations professionals if we didn't understand the importance of protecting our own reputation.

Once we know that we'll make a good team, the fun begins, and we get down to work.

BRAINSTORMING BASED ON RESEARCH

The first thing the team does is sit down with the client and zero in on what results we are trying to achieve. In the case of Dr. Smythe, we would be looking to raise awareness in the United States while promoting the product's benefits in anticipation of a formal launch. At the same time, we would be working to enhance Dr. Smythe's reputation as a respected nutritionist and scientist. We want consumers and doctors who might recommend his product to see him as the real thing. We would want to make sure he didn't get pulled down by the more unsavory aspects of the nutritional supplement market. Enhancing a reputation and guarding a reputation go hand in hand.

The team starts off by looking at the objectives and brainstorming ways to reach them. A lot of the brainstorming is based on consumer data. What demographic are we trying to reach? Who buys diet aids? Who looks for alternative ways to control cholesterol and blood sugar? What is the best way to reach them? Should we engage a spokesperson or work with an advocacy group? If so, who? What about influencers? We often spend a couple of hours just outlining the questions that need answering. After all, you can't find the answer if you don't know the question.

We then turn to consumer and scientific data to answer as many of our brainstorming questions as possible. The client will often have data to help us answer these questions, but if not, we can do our own research. We never want to create a campaign just because our gut says this is the right audience. We use research extensively to prove that this is the right audience.

The scientific data is also useful because often things hit us as natural differentiation points, which give us an immediate place to focus.

After this kickoff meeting, we usually give everyone a couple of days to marinate on the data. Or, if we need to do our own research, we set a realistic date in the future to reconvene. Then we come back together to brainstorm ideas to reach our goals. We won't solve everything in one brainstorm, but it gives us a good place to start and lets us see if there are any holes in our data.

In Dr. Smythe's case, we might decide that the tonic should be positioned as a high-end product, marketed to several different demographics. One would be upscale young professionals. We would talk about the tonic as an overall health supplement. The other would be more middle-aged consumers who are beginning to be concerned about cholesterol and diabetes. We would emphasize the tonic's benefits in these areas, though we'd need to be careful not to run afoul of the FDA with health claims. Of course, for both groups, the weight loss benefits would come into play. Who doesn't want a natural, easy way to lose a few pounds? A third demographic might be general practitioners and internists who are looking for nonprescription supplements to help their patients on the verge of diabetes or needing a cholesterol drug. As a secondary focus, we would also look to reach chiropractors. This physician group often touts vitamins and supplements to their patients, who are exactly the demographic groups we want to reach. The ultimate target in all demographic cohorts would be the type of consumer who prefers natural remedies to prescription drugs, though they don't reject Western medicine. Think the kind who drinks wheatgrass shots at Jamba Juice.

Once we pinpoint the target market (we work closely with the client's marketing and branding groups for this), we begin to throw out ideas to reach this target. This is where the real 360 degrees come into play. When I'm writing about the process, it will probably look like the steps are taken one after the other in a straight line. Actually, most steps are taken at the same time, often overlapping and circling and just generally interweaving with each other until the client is completely surrounded. Picture a ball of string with the client at the core. That is a 360-degree campaign. Our digital team will be working on the social media portion, while our communications specialists will be rounding up the press and looking for speaking spots on industry panels as well as appropriate TV shows. Depending on the product, we might also look for placement in movies and music videos.

TRADITIONAL PUBLIC RELATIONS

Social and digital media use up a lot of oxygen in the room, but traditional public relations is still the foundation of most campaigns. And the foundation of traditional public relations is messaging, positioning, and media relations. If we are going to pique journalists' and trade publication writers' interest in Dr. Smythe's tonic, we are going to have to grab their attention.

> *Social and digital media use up a lot of oxygen in the room, but traditional public relations is still the foundation of most campaigns.*

Americans have a love affair with all things Australian, from the accents to the koala bears. Focusing on Dr. Smythe's Australian roots would seem to be the perfect way to go. In addition to being a place Americans want to visit, it has a down-to-earth, "real" aura that would lend credibility to the tonic. If doctors and consumers in no-nonsense Australia swear by it, then it must be good.

We like to use press events to create interest in our clients. With a view of using the Australian connection, we might decide to host a cocktail party at the Bronx Zoo. We'd serve iconic Australian hors d'oeuvres such as pavlova, Tim Tams, and Anzac biscuits. We'd serve Australian beers and wines. We'd organize a private tour of the animal exhibits featuring Australian wildlife, such as the little blue penguin exhibit, which is at the Bronx Zoo in partnership with Sydney's Taronga Zoo, as well as the kangaroos, reptiles, and other native Australian fauna.

We'd use the walls of the pavilion to screen videos explaining the benefits of the tonic and how Dr. Smythe developed it. Testimonials from relatable celebrities or influencers or other third-party health experts would be good to include. Dr. Smythe would be in the middle of the event, speaking to reporters and presenting his tonic.

The guest list would be an eclectic mix of writers representing traditional, hard-copy trade publications and newspapers as well as writers for less traditional but influential blogs, online news sites, and social media influencers. We would also include the producers from the morning news and syndicated talk shows. Publications would cover the gamut from *Shape* to AARP's *The Magazine*, from *Prevention* to *USA Today*, and everything in between. For this particular campaign, we would be casting a very wide net, because the tonic would be of interest to a wide variety of cohorts.

Developing the invitation list is only half the battle. We need to turn those invites into bodies. The event is only as good as the people who actually attend, so when planning an event, we need to grab their attention and make the event too good to pass up from the very beginning. For Dr. Smythe, we would want something eye catching that sets our invite apart from all the others the reporters and trade publications are receiving. After a lot of brainstorming, we might come up with the idea of delivering stuffed kangaroos to each potential guest. The printed invite would be in the kangaroo's pouch along with a sample-size bottle of the tonic. Depending on our budget, we might even order bottles in the shape of baby kangaroos to hold the tonic sample and sit in the pouch with the invite. Using a stuffed animal to deliver the invitation has several advantages. First of all, it is sure to catch the eye of the recipient. How do you miss a stuffed kangaroo being delivered to your desk? It's likely to be the topic of talk around the newsroom, which creates a buzz around the event. A stuffed animal isn't something you throw away. Instead, it's likely to sit on your desk for several days, reinforcing the event. In addition, the stuffed-kangaroo-invitation campaign makes for great Instagram, Facebook, and other social media images. We might stage a photo with all the kangaroos piled on a couch in the lobby. Then we'd show a few peeking out the backpack of a bicycle courier. Other photos could show them being carried into a building and signing in at the front desk. Having a striking visual for the invitation raises awareness of the event in multiple ways that a simple emailed invite couldn't.

FINDING THE RIGHT SPOKESPERSON

Spokespeople are not a part of every campaign. Sometimes the products just don't lend themselves to celebrity endorsements, or there is an expert already in-house. An innovative medical device being marketed to surgeons would be better promoted on its own rather than spoken about by an actor, though a highly respected surgeon might work. But a consumer product such as Dr. Smythe's tonic is perfect for a spokesperson connection. In this case, we would look for someone to continue the Australian connection, and we might look for two if we didn't think we could find a single person who was relatable to all the targeted demographics. What do we look for in a spokesperson? Well, above all, they have to be relatable. We are going to be leveraging the spokesperson's reputation to enhance our product and unknown nutritionist. They have to be recognizable to your target audience. It doesn't help to have a spokesperson if your audience has no idea who they are. The spokesperson needs to encompass the characteristics and benefits that we are associating with the product. In this case, we'd be looking for healthy, outdoorsy, athletic, fun, and natural spokespeople. Age doesn't matter as much as the "healthiness" they exhibit. In fact, an older but young-looking, athletic, and attractive spokesperson is often better, because everyone wants to look younger than they are as they age. Some names that might get thrown into the mix are Toni Collette and Nicole Kidman (but not Keith Urban). If we want to be sportier, we would look at someone like Bindi Irwin, the daughter of the crocodile hunter Steve Irwin. If we wanted a little edgier, we might look to someone like Bethany Hamilton, the Hawaiian surfer who lost her arm in a shark attack. Although she's American, surfing and Australia go together like Dr. Smythe's tonic and a healthy lifestyle. The bottom line is that we want someone who can believably speak to the benefits of the tonic and make people think, "He or she looks great. I want to look like that / have energy like that / feel as healthy as that. If he or she uses the tonic and looks that great, I'm going to try it too."

THE INNOVATOR BEHIND THE INNOVATION

I've mentioned it before, but it bears mentioning again. I work almost exclusively with innovators who are making a difference in others' lives. Whatever their product or service, it is something that truly helps their target market. As such, it is important for the consumer or professional target audience (doctors, surgeons, dermatologists, aestheticians, etc.) to know the person behind the product. To trust a new product or service, consumers want to know that the person trying to improve their lives is the "real deal" and not some sort of snake oil salesman. To that end, we encourage our clients to accept invitations to appear on TV shows and sit on industry panels. We explain the importance of talking directly to writers at consumer and trade publications to get their story out there. But we don't toss them to the wolves unprepared. We have an entire training program that not only prepares clients to answer any question thrown at them but works with how to present that information. We work on how to stand or sit on stage. How to speak into a microphone and connect with the audience. How to look at the questioner. Even how to modulate their voice and use specific mannerisms to be pleasing and authoritative. Speaking to a crowd or in front of TV cameras typically does not come naturally, but we make sure our clients are prepared when presented with the opportunity. Once we know they are prepared, we work to get them in front of the right audiences. Dr. Smythe would be perfect for *The Dr. Oz Show*, *The Doctors*, morning syndicated shows, and maybe—the gold standard—a segment on the *TODAY* show or *Good Morning America*.

SOCIAL AND DIGITAL PUBLIC RELATIONS

Mentions in the press and on TV are great, but we also need to look at promoting Dr. Smythe via social media. As mentioned earlier, unlike most other public relations firms, we have a separate group skilled in digital public relations. This really is a different skill set from traditional public relations. We focus on our client, and to give the best service possible, a firm needs to provide both traditional and digital services.

In Dr. Smythe's case, our digital team would be looking to work with YouTube and Instagram influencers who are followed by our target audience. While the traditional public relations side looked for a more traditional spokesperson, the digital side would likely look for beauty and health influencers known to our target audience but likely less well known to the general public. We'd be trying to get the attention of popular bloggers, social media stars, and others with thousands or millions of followers. To tie in with the Bronx Zoo event, it would make sense to approach the people behind the Bronx Zoo's Cobra Twitter account and try to get them on board with sending out tweets about the event or Australians or health tonics or anything related. They might have a special affinity with the small blue penguins or Australian-based reptiles in the zoo. The Cobra is entertaining and would undoubtedly come up with something tweetworthy that would generate buzz around the event and Dr. Smythe. I don't think we've ever had a snake as an influencer before, but there is a first time for everything.

PLANNING FOR THE UNPLANNED

While most of our work is focused on raising awareness, controlling perceptions, and driving recommendations, we also need to be prepared if things go wrong. What happens if someone starts taking Dr. Smythe's tonic and has an adverse reaction? What happens if a competitor challenges the data from Australia and brands Dr. Smythe a quack and a grifter? What happens if someone taking Dr. Smythe's tonic dies suddenly? Even if it is unlikely that the death was caused by the tonic, rumors will spread on social media and be hard to stop. Or even what do we do if Dr. Smythe himself is discovered to have clogged arteries or diabetes-level blood sugar? This tonic is helpful, but it's not a miracle drug. These things happen. James Fixx, who started America's fitness craze, died of a heart attack while jogging at the age of 52. We need to have plans in place if the worst happens.

The way to plan for the unplanned is to brainstorm scenarios from mild—consumers don't like Dr. Smythe's voice and tune him out—to the tragic—someone using the tonic dies. While we

Having disaster plans for those white swans we can see makes it more likely that we'll have something that just needs tweaking if a black swan makes an appearance.

can't foresee everything, having plans in place for a variety of scenarios makes executing them quickly more possible. And having disaster plans for those white swans we can see makes it more likely that we'll have something that just needs tweaking if a black swan makes an appearance.

KFC did a marvelous job of using social media to handle a chicken supply crisis in the UK early in 2018. It managed to hit just the right tone in its response—not too serious, not too cavalier. First of all, it quickly activated its social media team to acknowledge the problem and engage irritated customers. Companies sometimes give in to their impulse to make light of customers' annoyance. After all, we are only talking about being unable to have a chicken leg with mashed potatoes one day. We aren't talking about a life-and-death situation, like a hospital running out of antibiotics. There was undoubtedly a taco or burger chain across the street.

Instead of ignoring the problem, however, the social media team immediately jumped on Twitter to apologize and let consumers know what was happening. This alone went a long way toward mollifying followers. Then, KFC had the good fortune of having Iceland Foods, a supplier of frozen foods to restaurant chains, chime in with frenemy tweets offering to supply the KFC fast food outlets with frozen chicken. Iceland Foods' celebrity spokesperson, Peter Andre, briefly entered the fray, drawing more attention to the feed. Tower Hamlets' police station tweeted, "Please do not contact us about the #KFCCrisis—it is not a police matter if your favourite eatery is not serving the menu that you desire." Burger King jumped in with a tongue-in-cheek offer to help disappointed KFC patrons. Soon, people were reading the Twitter feed for the fun of it and to see who else might respond rather than to vent. Through it all, the social media team responded with grace, keeping everyone informed while engaging in good-humored bantering.

The next day, KFC ran a full-page ad in local papers that started out with the headline, "We're Sorry." It continued, "A chicken restaurant without any chicken. It's not ideal."

The apology was well received. But what caught everyone's eye was the half-page picture above the "We're Sorry" headline of an empty KFC bucket with the letters rearranged to spell FCK.

The ad won the internet that day. Now, instead of talking about a lack of chicken and screwed-up distribution systems, the UK (and the world) was talking about the brilliant response. It was a perfect class in crisis management.

The key here is preparation. There is no way KFC could have had that quick a response, and that perfect a response, without preparation. I'm sure that at some time a session took place where the public relations team brainstormed worst-case scenarios and someone said, "What do we do if we don't have any chicken?" After everyone stopped laughing at such a preposterous scenario, they got to work and prepared a response to sit on the shelf, ready for the time when just such an incident might occur.

NEVER ENDING

A public relations campaign is not just a one-time—or a one-month or one-year—project. Growing a product's share of voice requires continuous attention. We regularly analyze what we are doing for a client and determine what changes should be made. For Dr. Smythe, these changes might involve pulling in more American testimonials as the product gained traction in the US. We likely would look to add target audiences and work with the marketing department to expand distribution channels. With every new market, we'd develop a new campaign. We probably wouldn't need to start from scratch, but each change in marketing direction would require changes in public relations direction.

And just as we are beginning to feel that we are coming to the end of a campaign, the client will often want to introduce a new product or a new use for an existing product, and we all jump in and begin anew. As long as a client has a product in the market, the need for public relations and digital marketing never ends.

As you read this chapter, I hope you got an idea of how many t's must be crossed and i's dotted to put together a successful campaign. And this chapter was just a surface overview. There is so much more to running multiple public relations and social media campaigns while also overseeing the ins and outs of growing EvolveMKD. Plus, of course, I want to change the industry for the better.

Meeting with prospective clients, being available to existing clients, sitting down with my team to develop successful campaigns, meeting with accountants and lawyers and other professionals needed to run a business, making the decisions on which paths to take as the business grows, finding time for myself and my family—it can all be overwhelming. In the end, however, it all boils down to setting priorities and being brave enough to make the decisions that have to be made. That makes it sound simpler than it really is, but the next couple of chapters will walk you through how I balance it all and how a few of my methods might help you as well.

CHALLENGE **ACCEPTED**

Client: Specialty pharma company creating facial injectables for dermatologists and plastic surgeons.

Challenge: Increase utilization of the injectable by men by highlighting the procedure as a regular part of a man's grooming routine. Develop a strategic campaign to generate a steady stream of consumer media highlighting men's grooming and injectable treatments.

What EvolveMKD did: Hit the road in an Airstream-turned-mobile barbershop, seeking out top media and influencers to make them aware that injectables can be an important part of a man's grooming regimen. This multicity media event included stops at all the major New York City and Los Angeles publishing houses and broadcast outlets, where editors and on-air media were treated to haircuts, hot shaves, and injections. Additionally, multiple influencers blogged about their experiences and utilized social media to drive traffic to the campaign.

Result: Captured the looked-for attention, earning featured write-ups in outlets such as the *New York Times*, *Esquire*, and AskMen.com. And the coverage continues—to date, this campaign has garnered almost 300 million impressions. Making use of the Airstream while it was in New York City, 40 tri-state-area healthcare providers got a sneak peek at this new advertising campaign at an evening event following the media blitz.

CHAPTER 5

BE #BRAVE

When I launched EvolveMKD, I knew I wanted to grow a company that did things differently—did things the right way, as far as I was concerned. I had a pretty good idea of how I wanted that to look, but I didn't have a total grasp of what it would take to make it happen.

There are a thousand moving parts when it comes to launching a company, from developing a business plan to hiring accountants and lawyers to choosing a place to house everyone to differentiating EvolveMKD from other public relations and social media firms to bringing on team members to . . . well, you get the picture.

Turns out running a company isn't just about providing a service. In fact, the service itself might be the least of my worries. To have a chance at creating a growing, thriving business, I have to make smart decisions. I also have to be brave enough to act on those decisions, even if it sometimes means jumping across—or into—the abyss.

With decision-making being so crucial—it is, essentially, the primary job of a CEO—you'd think there would be guidelines that help ensure good decisions. Turns out there are indeed guidelines. Lots of guidelines—lots of different, sometimes contradictory guidelines. Trying to decide which model to follow is as much of a decision as the decisions they are purporting to help you make.

There are people who have spent a lot more time on quantifying decision-making than I have. There are entire college and corporate classes on it. In fact, I took one in college. It was interesting, but I sometimes wonder if studying decision-making really changes how people approach problems. I suspect we all fall back on a combination of intuition, gut, and facts we have on hand rather than solely relying on spreadsheets, objective metrics, and decision-making models.

These classes often start with a basic, classical, or rational model. This model assumes the manager making the decision is rational and logical, has all the data at hand, and will make a decision in the best interests of the organization. Another model is based on the premise that managers do not always make rational decisions, nor do they always make decisions in the best interests of the company. They just don't have time to look at all options. Instead, they go for the first acceptable solution, even if it is not the best. Given my hectic schedule, I fully understand this impulse. Sometimes I just need to make a decision and move on.

Others say it isn't that complicated. People simply make the decision they want to make based on experience and intuition and then try to find objective reasons that will justify it afterward. Sounds about right to me.

For a less academic approach, walk into any bookstore (or, more likely, go on Amazon), and look at the hundreds of books on decision-making. Most are targeted to the business community, but some, like *Thinking Fast and Slow,* by Daniel Kahneman, or *Blink: The Power of*

Thinking Without Thinking, by Malcolm Gladwell, or *The Black Swan: The Impact of the Highly Improbable,* by Nassim Nicholas Taleb, have become consumer best sellers. It's clear that business leaders need help making smart decisions, but your everyday coffee drinker is also looking for help, even if it is just in choosing the best coffee shop.

What does all this tell us? It tells me there is no single, best way to make decisions. If there were, we'd all be using it or maybe programming our artificial intelligence system to make unerringly rational, optimized decisions. But it doesn't work that way.

So, how do I make smart decisions? And how do I decide which abyss to jump into and which to run from? Good questions.

For me, decision-making is highly personal. Sometimes the path is clear, and the right decision is obvious. Sometimes it takes lots and lots of time and data. Sometimes it's simply down and dirty, let's get this done right now. Still other times, it's a highly rational process. Not only is there no single way for everyone to make decisions, there isn't even a single way for *me* to make decisions.

> *Not only is there no single way for everyone to make decisions, there isn't even a single way for me to make decisions.*

I generally follow a broad process where first I identify the problem. It seems pretty obvious to me that you can't solve a problem if you haven't defined it. I also make sure I have a specific goal in mind. Goals give me direction. If I know where I want to end up, it's easier to decide on the steps to get there. If I need more information to make an informed decision, I gather the data I need. When I feel relatively confident that I have all the information I need, I make the decision and rarely look back.

Probably the first truly major decision of my life was where to go to college. Before that, decisions were more in the "training" category, where I was making relatively low-risk decisions—what clothes to wear, what boy to date, what sports to play—in preparation for the day I'd have to make a really life-changing decision. College was it.

Many high school students are able to target a limited number of colleges because they already know what they want to major in and so focus on universities that are well known in those fields. Or maybe they have always wanted to go to their mom's or dad's alma mater. I didn't have those restrictions. I had no idea what I wanted to major in, and while my parents went to a good college, I wasn't drawn to it. That meant I had the entire universe of colleges to choose from. I obviously needed to narrow those options. I decided to base my choice on academics as well as where I could continue my athletic career. The factors that went into this decision were intuitive rather than rational. I just knew I would be happiest at a well-known academic institution. I also felt I'd be happiest staying near a major city. I'm from New Jersey and was born in Brooklyn, so I grew up going to New York City regularly. Now that I'd narrowed my choices somewhat, I applied to several that fit the requirements and ended up accepting the best one that accepted me. It worked out great.

Score one for intuitive decision-making.

CHALLENGE **ACCEPTED**

Client: Innovative aesthetic procedure.

Challenge: Introduce key media and influencers to the company and its breakthrough innovation to the European market.

What EvolveMKD did: Invited top-tier media and influencers in key European markets to join us in Paris to learn about the one-of-a-kind treatment. The event featured a panel of physicians who had conducted clinical studies for the treatment as well as a patient who shared her firsthand experience. The celebration of the launch continued with an intimate dinner and a show at the iconic Moulin Rouge.

Result: Garnered instant social media posts surrounding the news with nearly 20,000 social media impressions within 24 hours. Secured placements in top-tier European media outlets, including *InStyle Spain Online, Vanity Fair Italia Online,* and *La Pelle* (Italy), resulting in 3 million impressions.

OVERCOMING FEAR

Decision-making actually has two equal parts: making the decision and then executing. Until you put your decision into practice, it's all theoretical.

Choosing a college—and being brave enough to be the first in my family to go out of state—was actually pretty easy compared to the decision to start EvolveMKD, but the process was similar. My goal was to move on from the partnership position I held at a small agency. That was a harder decision than you might imagine. The partnership wasn't working, but I'm not one to give up. I kept thinking I should be able to fix it. It was my lawyer who said to me, "Look, we could patch this. We could put a Band-Aid on it, but we're heading to the same conclusion whether it's now or years from now." He pointed out that I had the most power at that point in time. That made me refocus not on trying to fix things but on what my viable options were.

Looking at my options, it appeared I had three: I could join a big agency, but I'd done that before and felt I wasn't really a good fit. I could join a smaller agency and eventually become a partner, but that might put me in the same situation I was in at the time. Or I could start my own. I suppose staying as a partner in my current agency was a fourth option, but like the options on *House Hunters*, I crossed that out right at the beginning. When something isn't working, it's best to cut your losses and move on quickly to something that is or could be working.

When weighing the options, I first focused on the positives. What were the advantages of running my own agency versus joining someone else's? The main advantage of starting my own firm was that I could do things my way. (I normally think that my way is the best way.) I could provide services to clients the way I believed they should be provided. I could treat my team (and myself) the way professionals deserved to be treated. The main advantage to joining another agency was that I would have a support system and financial security from the beginning. Knowing where your next paycheck is coming from is not an insignificant advantage.

Conversely, the disadvantage of starting my own business was the lack of security found in joining an established agency. I might very well find myself a year out with a failed venture. The disadvantage of going with an ongoing firm was that I'd done that before, and it wasn't a good fit. If I wasn't happy, chances were good that a year out I'd find myself back where I started—debating starting my own firm or joining yet another company.

My husband finally put everything into perspective for me. I kept saying to him, "But there's no guarantee this will work. How am I going to be different? Does the world need another public relations and social media agency?"

He responded, "But it will be different because of you. What's the worst-case scenario? The worst-case scenario is you get no clients. So, you do it for a year and fail. Then you can just get another job. You will go into a job interview, and when they ask, 'Oh, what'd you do with this year?' you'll be able to say, 'I tried to open up a business.' No one's going to say, 'Wow, we're not going to hire her!' People are going to say, 'Wow, that's amazing.'"

I looked at him and said, "Well, when you put it that way, I guess it doesn't sound as scary."

My intuition and gut as well as friends and colleagues had all been telling me to go with my own firm. But it was my husband who finally tipped the scales when he said, "What is the worst that could happen if you start your own firm? You fail, and you get on with another company in a year or so. Nothing really lost."

That was a totally liberating way to look at this huge decision I was making. Could I live with the worst-case scenario? Yes, I could. So yes, I did.

> *Could I live with the worst-case scenario? Yes, I could. So yes, I did.*

Since then, I've incorporated that question into all my major decision-making. It's certainly important to weigh pros and cons, but in the end, the real question is, What is the worst thing that can happen if I choose option A or option B, and can I live with it?

I also ask myself, "What is the worst that will happen if I don't do this?" Deciding not to decide is a decision in itself.

Looking back now, being brave enough to start my own business was probably the scariest decision I've had to make but the one that in reality had the least consequences. I've had to make decisions that had much higher consequences now that I have overhead and people and I'm responsible for their jobs. Nearly every decision I make now has consequences that are much greater than the one that resulted in EvolveMKD, but those decisions seem much less scary than that decision.

I guess I don't fit into the classic decision model, where managers are always rational, because every decision after that first one has seemed less daunting, yet many have much more of a potential downside. For example, the next major decision after deciding to open the business was deciding to rent office space. This should have been much scarier than deciding to go into business for myself because renting space involved a personal guarantee and a huge check. Worst-case scenario was pretty bad. But it still wasn't as terrifying to me as opening the business, even though signing a lease can have much bigger financial implications for a long time.

One of the major decisions I have to make regularly is whether to take on a new client. We have a set of guidelines for clients—they must be innovators, must be willing to see us as a partner, must treat the EvolveMKD team with respect, and so on. But sometimes other factors enter into the equation. In the beginning, the need for consistent cash flow was a huge factor. We needed cash flow, and clients mean cash flow. Today, as we have reached a stable critical mass, cash flow is still important, but I feel more confident turning down a client that I'm not totally happy with. In fact, I find it much easier to turn down a client that doesn't meet our guidelines than to sever the relationship with one that is already on board and paying their bills, even if I've found them to be difficult, possibly just this side of abusive. Dropping a current, bill-paying client means I need to replace those revenues.

I then ask myself, "What is the worst that will happen?"

If I sever the relationship, the worst that will happen is that EvolveMKD will not be able to grow as projected. We won't go out of business, and we won't have to lay off members of our team, but our growth could come to a screeching halt if I don't replace those revenues quickly.

If I decide to keep the client, the worst that will happen is that I will lose valued team members who would rather quit than handle that account any further. Although no one is indispensable, every member of our team was chosen for specific skills as well as a work style and personality that enhance the entire organization. Losing a team member because of working conditions is unacceptable.

I have my decision. I want the team members to stay, so the difficult client needs to go.

Visualizing the worst-case scenario and deciding if I can live with it has made implementing my decisions much easier. It's made me brave enough to make the moves I know I need to make—hire top-notch executives, rent larger office space, expand services to meet clients' needs—but might have hesitated too long if I were relying solely on spreadsheet metrics.

Making smart decisions is as much avoiding bad decisions as it is making good ones—maybe more. Warren Buffett is quoted as saying, "You only have to do a very few things right in your life, so long as you don't do too many things wrong." I interpret this to mean that if you avoid the downside, you'll end up successful. And who can argue with Warren Buffett?

As mentioned earlier, one of the major recurring decisions I have to make is whether to take on a new client. Avoiding doing too many things wrong when it comes to expanding our client base usually comes down to making sure we vet the client first. A few things always get my spidey sense twitching.

CLIENT RED FLAGS

- If a client has switched agencies a lot in a short period of time, that means the client is the problem, not the agencies.

- If someone has completely unrealistic expectations, we just say no.

- If during the conversation they display an unwillingness to listen to a different perspective or think that they are better than the next person, that's a huge warning sign, because they're never going to listen to us.

- If the client's budget is $20, and they want the world—not worth it.

- If we don't think the product or the technology is credible or we just don't like the brand, that's another reason we say no.

- We definitely decline to take on clients that I know will drag down team morale or will not be a partner with us.

I might need more clients to fund EvolveMKD's growth, but I will never accept an unethical client (think someone who exaggerates or lies about the benefits of a product or overcharges consumers) or one with a product I consider harmful (think tobacco) or a firm that uses cruel methods to test its products. Those are the easy decisions. But not everything is that clear cut.

One of the things we've learned to watch for is conflict of interest, and sometimes turning away those clients isn't such an easy decision. I'm focused on a relatively niche universe of innovators. We need to be careful that we don't take on a client that will compete with a current client. When I started in public relations, it was easier to see conflicts. Now it's murkier, because a lot of my clients have products with a variety of purposes that can be used by or marketed to a myriad of audiences.

Certain kinds of accounts aren't even real conflicts, but they would put us in a weird spot. So, for instance, we would never take on individual doctors, because we work with so many physicians through our brands that it would be a little bit unethical for us, at least in my opinion. It's not really a conflict, but how could we work with a big pharma company that works with multiple dermatologists, and we have one that's paying us?

I recently had to say no to two people whom I really like very much personally and who I know are good clients, but their business would conflict with that of current clients. One is definitely a conflict. The other one would just make other clients uncomfortable, so it wasn't worth it. One of these clients would have been a $700,000 account. Saying no to that one was truly painful. But I need to keep the long term in mind. So, while it would be nice in the short term to have that infusion of cash, long term it was going to negatively impact EvolveMKD's reputation. It's just not worth it.

At the end, we only take on clients that we are happy to work with and proud to represent. As a public relations and social media firm, it's just as important for us to protect our own reputation as it is to promote our clients'.

> *It's just as important for us to protect our own reputation as it is to promote our clients'.*

Finally, I take into consideration whether the team wants to work on the account. Some clients come in with very small budgets, but they have a sexy brand, and the team wants to take them on. I might have rejected them as clients, but if my team is gung ho, then great. Godspeed.

Even with all this due diligence, things sometimes don't work out. That's life. But we try to at least set ourselves up for success by being disciplined in what we'll take.

PEOPLE MATTER

It's the decisions that involve my team that are the hardest to make. I can decide to move the office into a larger space at my morning exercise class. I can decide to add a new line of services over tea with my exec team. I can determine what to charge a new client while on the way to the airport. But when it comes to making decisions that could affect team members, I agonize. When it comes to people's livelihoods, I have to get it right.

For example, I mentioned earlier that I think it's important to provide top-tier benefits, including health insurance, to my staff. If I want to hire top-notch professionals, and I do, then I need to make sure they are taken care of. Providing top-of-the-line insurance and paying 100 percent of the cost was relatively easy in the beginning, when I had just a few employees. As we've grown, however, the cost of covering 100 percent of the insurance premiums became onerous. I just couldn't afford it.

This isn't an option A or option B decision. It's much more nuanced. I could decide to continue to provide insurance as before, knowing that I would need to skimp in other areas of the company. Or I could decide to cover 100 percent of a less desirable plan, knowing some of my team members might be relying on benefits that would not be available in the cheaper plan. Or I could continue to offer the top-notch plan, but only cover a portion, knowing that for some employees, picking up their portion of the cost would impact other areas of their lives. And if I only covered a portion, how much would I cover?

The thing that makes decisions involving people so difficult is that an added layer must be considered: ethics and morality. Few ethical considerations go into expanding the office space. I suppose you want to make sure neither you nor the landlord is getting cheated, and maybe you want to make sure there are public transportation options nearby to reduce the burden on team members, but leasing new space is a pretty straightforward decision. But deciding to reduce health benefits, eliminate a line of services that will result in needing fewer team members, or taking on a client that will require the team to work countless late nights and early mornings are on an entirely different level.

Making decisions that affect my staff aren't all huge and angst producing. But even smaller decisions with very little downside can have a huge impact on morale and the way an employee feels about working at EvolveMKD. In addition to decisions revolving around foundational corporate responsibilities, such as compensation and benefits, I also need to make decisions on what perks we'll offer and what activities we'll sponsor. You hear about start-ups that offer public transportation passes or discounts for local parking garages. Some help with day care or provide chef-prepared meals. I want to make sure that whatever perks and benefits we offer fit into the type of culture I want to promote. For example, we've had experts come in to talk about customer service, the financial system, and other topics that aren't strictly public relations focused but that broaden the team's knowledge on various pieces of the business that are important to our clients.

In the end, it all comes down to people. It comes down to taking business personally. What perks would I have liked when I was working for other agencies? What would have made my life easier?

My team and I put in long hours. That's simply the nature of public relations. To make it easier for my team to balance work and life, I offer unlimited vacation days and sick leave. Why should people lose pay if their illness lasts longer than the five days most companies allow or if they need to stay with a sick parent longer than whatever personal-time-off days they have left? Responsible adults should be able to balance their work and life themselves. I know I would have liked that ability when I was working for others, so I'm providing it for my team. Life is so much more than social media campaigns.

One of our most talked-about perks is our annual Family Night. This event was a spin-off of a brainstorm session when we were talking about Bring Your Kids to Work Day. People started talking about how they didn't have kids but that they'd love their parents to come to work to see what they did all day. Others thought they'd like to include partners. The event soon morphed into Family Night, where the staff could invite anyone important to them—parents, in-laws, partners, extended family, kids, and so on—to spend the evening at the office and see what EvolveMKD is all about. We spend the majority of our day at work, but most of our families really know very little about our jobs and the people we spend most of our time with. The people working at EvolveMKD took a leap of faith when they came to work for my start-up agency. Nearly all of them were already top performers at other agencies or firms and didn't have to leave that stability to come to EvolveMKD. But they did come, and I wanted to show them how much I appreciated that leap as well as show their families that we'd arrived. I wanted their family members to know they made the right choice by coming to work for a start-up—we all know that our families worry about us, no matter how old or well established we are. We also wanted family members to experience some of the fun perks we have in the office. Because we're an aesthetic wellness and beauty agency, we provide eyebrow shaping as a perk, so we had that. We had a celebrity makeup artist doing women's makeup and recommending skin care and makeup products, and everyone got a very nice gift bag.

Family Night has turned out to be a huge hit with both the team members and their families. It's already become a summer tradition.

Maybe we should look into having a similar get-together during the winter holidays. Gotta put on my decision-making hat again.

CHALLENGE **ACCEPTED**

Client: Innovative medical procedure.

Challenge: Launch the innovative, FDA-approved system and develop a strategic campaign to generate a steady stream of news surrounding the launch during year one.

What EvolveMKD did: Took over a museum that was featuring a relevant exhibit and hosted a cocktail party reception that offered private tours of the exhibit to further celebrate the launch and the human form. An interactive photo booth and a performance from the Bumbys also provided attendees with an honest and cheeky appraisal of their appearance. More than seventy top-tier national media, physicians, client employees, board members, and analysts attended to learn more about this category-creating technology story.

Result: Immediate coverage, including TIME.com, MensHealth.com, MSN.com, and a segment on *The Doctors* as well as brand awareness on social media, generating nearly 300 million impressions. Also served as a reputation management tool with the financial community and key physician customers. Total results since the January 2017 launch exceed 500 million impressions across print, broadcast, online, and social media and a total ad value of nearly $7 million.

IT'S ALWAYS PERSONAL

People will tell you not to take the business of business personally. But I do take it personally. This is my business. It is me. Every decision, every misstep, and every success is me. So yes, I take it personally. And in doing that, I overlay my personal values and ethics onto my decisions. Spreadsheets and models aren't going to take those into account. Decisions for my company have to be decisions I'm happy with personally. This is the core of what makes EvolveMKD different. If I'm to run a company, it needs to be ethical. It needs to put people above profits. I will always put my team above the bottom line. I will always take the impact on my team into consideration. As long as that is the basis of any decision, it will be a smart decision.

I can't believe every public relations and social media agency doesn't come from a place of people first—encouraging a sustainable workforce would seem to be a no-brainer—but I know they don't. And that is to the detriment of the industry.

Although I've never run into a worst-case scenario, not all my decisions have turned out to be trouble-free. For example, early in the beginning, I had the chance to represent a very well known client. There were a lot of red flags—they'd been with several agencies, they had the reputation for not listening to their public relations people and then blaming them when things went wrong, the person who ran the product line that I'd represent was difficult—just a lot of things that gave me a bad feeling. But I still I took them on because they were a name, and I thought they would be helpful for us. Plus, others whom I respected thought it would be good for EvolveMKD to be associated with such a high-profile client so early in our existence.

They were worse than everything I had heard. They were worse than anything I could have imagined. It's one of the only times since opening that I had team members crying because the client was abusive. We can all deal with tough clients. This was an abusive client. There is a big difference.

I learned an important lesson here. I need to trust myself when it comes to what is best for my business. The times I've ignored my gut instincts or gone against what I felt was right because someone I thought knew better was promoting a different decision have almost universally turned out badly.

But the key to making smart decisions is to just keep going. Practice may not make perfect, but it certainly makes things easier. Michael Jordan was great at this. He has noted that he's missed more than nine thousand shots in his career. He missed the game-winning shot twenty-six times. Yet he still called for the ball. Jordan doesn't focus on the shots he's missed; he focuses on the ones he's made. You can't win if you aren't brave enough to try.

One of the challenges I've faced over and over—and just kept going—was resistance to my role as a female business owner. I have, of course, heard stories of women being asked to have a male cosigner or business partner in order to get financing, but I thought those were stories of a bygone era—until it happened to me.

EvolveMKD has been profitable since the beginning, and each year I've had to move the office to larger quarters to accommodate our growth. One year, I made offers on four separate spaces before one was accepted. I was competing with well-funded tech companies, which landlords seemed to be favoring even though they weren't profitable. But as frustrating as having my offers rejected was, this paled in comparison to finally getting an offer accepted only to have the landlord's attorney ask for my husband to act as a guarantor. This was not his company. It was mine. Would I have been asked to guarantee his lease agreement? I think not.

I've also found it incredibly challenging to get credit-line increases from my bank. This has less to do (probably nothing to do) with my being a woman and more to do with the amount of time my business has been in business. Yet I look around and see these same banks increasing credit lines for unprofitable tech firms. How does that work? And yes, I take these rejections personally.

This is where "making it happen" comes into play. Once I make a decision—we need to increase our credit line to keep up with our growth—I find a way to make it happen. In this case, I've had to change banks every year to get that credit-line increase. But I've done it and will do it again if I need to.

FUTURE PLANNING

EvolveMKD has been growing so fast that I've often felt I haven't had the time to plan for the future, but it's important I do so. Decisions need to be made, and the time to make a decision is before you have to. One of those decisions that need to be made before it is needed is EvolveMKD's exit strategy. Talking about an exit strategy before the firm is even five years old might seem strange, but how I envision the end game will determine our growth strategy. A company that is happy to stay at $10 million in revenues is very different from a company that is working toward $100 million annually. A company that I expect to run well into my retirement years will be very different from one that I'm positioning to be acquired or become the niche arm of a huge global enterprise.

Deciding on what the future will look like prevents misunderstandings down the road—and misunderstandings in a business setting are never good. I have an acquaintance who was part of the dot-com boom back in the 1990s. The start-up he was with had a very good offer on the table from a *Fortune* 50 corporation that wished to buy the tech firm, but the two founders couldn't agree on whether to accept it or not. They had never formalized where they saw the company going. One had always assumed they were positioning themselves to be acquired; the other thought they were in it for the long term. In the end, the offer was withdrawn, and the two have not spoken to each other since—which made it hard to run the company. It eventually was sold to another firm for a smidgen of the original offer. A simple exit strategy—"We want to sell this company for this many dollars. We want to retain this percentage of control. If we get an offer that meets those parameters, we will sell"; or "We want to hold this company forever and pass it down to our children"—would have saved the company and their friendship. I want to make sure I have a firm idea of where I want to be before I have to make a decision on which path to take.

EvolveMKD is in a good place right now. We're profitable and growing. We're large enough that we can offer big-agency-quality services yet small enough that I can personally be involved with each client. There will come a time, however, when our growth trajectory takes us to the size at which I'll no longer be able to take every client's phone call. Do I want that? Do I want to give up the personal interaction that I've thrived on to this point? What's my end game?

Those are all questions I'm still wrestling with. And yes, I'm using my husband's line: "What's the worst that will happen?" Using this question and my own judgment will get me to where I want to be, but I'm not there yet. Stay tuned.

CHAPTER 6

IT'S ALL IN THE # PRIORITIES

t's obvious that not every task is equally important. But I have a personality that wants to get it all done. Crucial, unimportant, completely off topic—I want to add it all to my list and not stop until I've checked everything off. But it's never done, is it? The minute I check one item off my list, another is added. Frankly, another is often added before I even start checking things off.

This is where prioritization comes in.

I didn't always prioritize the activities in my day . . . or my life or my job. I just somehow got it all done—or drove myself crazy trying. Everything seemed to have the same level of importance or at least seemed just as important to do. But as my career began to take off, I found my job taking over my life. I was working harder than ever. Putting in more hours than anyone else. Yet the more I worked, the less I seemed to accomplish, because my list kept growing longer. Life was getting out of control. Something had to change.

I needed to set priorities. EvolveMKD would never have come to fruition if I hadn't figured out what really needed doing and how to focus on it. Taking charge of my time allowed me to focus on what is important and minimize stress—which is still not very minimal given I'm CEO of a successful public relations firm.

I remember exactly when I figuratively said, "Enough!" and grabbed my life back. It was two agencies ago. I was going through some really major life changes—it was a year to remember, for sure.

Because of those life changes (let's call it what it was: life chaos), I decided to see a therapist to help me sort through everything that was happening and regain my footing. I firmly believe that professionals are put into this world for a purpose, and we should all take advantage of their expertise, whether it is an acupuncturist (whom I also have a standing appointment with), management consultant, lawyer, house cleaner, trainer, or therapist. To make time for this weekly appointment, I told my manager that I had to leave every Wednesday at 6:00 p.m. Full stop. Nonnegotiable.

And you know what? Everyone just said, "Okay." The world didn't come to a screeching halt. Clients didn't abandon the agency in droves. Work wasn't left undone. Life went on. And it went on much more rationally, because I decided to prioritize something that was important to me.

When I was recruited by the agency before EvolveMKD, I let them know right from the start that I had a couple of standing appointments that meant I needed to leave work early. In addition, I was about to get engaged and wanted to start working out prior to the wedding. These sessions would also be during the traditional workday. I'm a responsible overachiever who is willing to work 24/7, so all I was asking in return was the flexibility to manage my own schedule. In other words, to be treated as an adult. Shockingly, my future partner totally agreed. I seemed to be the only one who felt it was a big ask to put myself first.

Making myself a priority has paid dividends I couldn't foresee when I first made the move. When my partnership started going south, it was my daily exercise sessions that kept me sane. I wasn't allowed back in the office for the final six weeks of my partnership, but I couldn't start my own business because we hadn't signed the separation agreement yet. The stress was unreal. The only thing that got me through that period was exercise. Instead of standing around waiting for the lawyer to call, I would run to the gym or run to a class, and it really helped to keep me sane. So, as EvolveMKD got underway, I knew I had to prioritize exercise to prioritize myself.

In our hard-driving American culture, saying that exercise is a priority somehow sounds frivolous. But I recently heard that for a business owner, not exercising is the same as choosing stress and depression. Exercise, beyond the physical benefits, provides space away from the work and an opportunity to gain mental clarity. A calm, clear business owner is certainly better for employees and clients than a stressed-out, uptight decision-maker.

At this point, I know you are thinking, "Well, that's easy for you to say. But I just have way too many things to do. I just can't find the time for myself." I hear that all the time, even from my own colleagues. The day has the same number of hours for me as for you, and if I can find the time, you can too. You just have to resolve to do it.

In fact, I'd argue that you can't afford not to find time for yourself.

CHALLENGE **ACCEPTED**

Client: High-end china and flatware company.

Challenge: Reinvigorate the brand to make entertaining at home accessible and fun for a US millennial audience.

What EvolveMKD did: Identified unique partnership opportunities with culinary and wine experts and influencers to highlight the evolution of the brand from your grandma's china to a modern, must-have line for everyone's home.

Result: Over 875 million impressions across long-lead and short-lead media including *Good Housekeeping*, *Veranda*, ElleDecor.com, NYMag.com, Brides.com, and CNTraveler.com. Garnered more than 8.6 million social media impressions as a result of top lifestyle influencer brand mentions. Content received an average 2.7 percent engagement rate.

BUSINESS PRIORITIES

While prioritizing myself is my prime priority, the main reason I need to take care of myself is so that I can give my best to EvolveMKD. I have people who rely on me for their livelihood. I'm not participating as an individual in a triathlon or skateboard competition, where a loss only affects me. I'm a team captain, and my poor play can result in a loss affecting every member of my team.

I see my life divided into equally important portions encompassing personal and work. My work life probably takes up more than its fair share of my time and mental space, but because it is so satisfying, I'm good with that. Within my personal life, I prioritize exercise and other self-care activities. In my work life, I prioritize the activities that will move EvolveMKD forward—securing new clients, keeping current clients happy, creating an ethical work environment for my team. These are big, high-impact priorities, but if I'm not careful, I can find myself drowning in minutia and spending too much time on activities that are personally satisfying but not very important. Or maybe not even satisfying, just nagging, like keeping my email box uncluttered.

To help me prioritize, I've created a mental image of EvolveMKD where the company is a boat floating on a sea of soap bubbles. Each bubble is an important activity that keeps the company afloat. If any of these bubbles burst, the boat would be rocked and possibly even sink. Smaller bubbles swirl around and enhance the picture but wouldn't cause the company to sink if they popped. Surrounding it all and holding the bubbles together is a force field labeled "integrity."

Integrity is the overarching theme for everything EvolveMKD does. This sends us back to the earlier chapters, when I talked about doing things differently. It would be disingenuous to claim that the bottom line isn't crucial to the survival of EvolveMKD. But I believe—in fact, I know—that basing decisions on ethical factors enhances that bottom line in a sustainable way. When you look at life through an ethical lens, you don't have to worry that a decision made today will come back to bite you down the road. You don't have to worry about your reputation, and you don't have to worry that your company is built on shifting

I always prioritize solutions that positively impact my team or clients, even if I take a short-term hit to my bottom line. In the long run, I know integrity will win out.

sands. If you put your people and your clients first, everything will fall into place. I always prioritize solutions that positively impact my team or clients, even if I take a short-term hit to my bottom line. In the long run, I know integrity will win out.

Once I prioritized integrity as the overarching EvolveMKD

theme, I could dig a little deeper and look at actionable priorities—those bubbles holding up the company.

As my life has become more complicated, I've been doing a lot of thinking about priorities (hence this chapter), and I think, for me, it comes down to making success a priority. I know that sounds really squishy and bumper stickerish, but it just means concentrating on things that promote success and letting other things play second fiddle. It means being laser focused on finding ways to succeed and not letting roadblocks stop you. That fits me to a T. Remember way back in the beginning of the book when I mentioned that I always won the Most Improved Player award? I'm a plugger. I might not be the best when I start out, but I just keep working at it until I reach the top. I approach running EvolveMKD in the same way. I might not know exactly what I'm doing all the time, but I'm going to keep working at it until I do.

Just as I think work-life balance is a really personal equation, what constitutes success for you and how you prioritize work to make it happen is personal. For me, success is less about making money and more about having a great life surrounded by a great community and support network. To get there, I need to run EvolveMKD with integrity and with core values that focus on people. But to keep things humming along, I need to actually get tasks done, not just talk about it.

People, of course, are a prime priority. Ask any business owner what keeps them up at night, and they'll say, "Meeting payroll." How do I know that? Because when I was doing my due diligence before launching EvolveMKD, I surveyed everyone I could find who ran their own company and asked about their worst-case scenario. Each and every one of them, without exception, said they broke into cold sweats when things got so tight that they thought they might miss payroll. My team depends on me to pay my bills so they can pay theirs.

Because protecting my team is so important, actions that promote a positive cash flow are always high priority.

Thus, I've been very conservative in hiring, because I don't want to ever feel like I'm on the edge of a cliff (remember: avoid worst-case scenarios). We are probably a bit short staffed, but EvolveMKD is not a sweatshop. It does mean, however, that I sometimes need to do the work of three people, but as I said before, I like to work. And it's my company, so I don't mind (in fact, I like the control, so it's really not a hardship).

Making payroll means I need to make sure the company is healthy, and so I set priorities in my business life just as I do in my personal life. As Americans, we tend to believe that hard work is the key to success. Many (most?) successful business owners and strategists will politely disagree. For them, it's all about focusing on the high-priority items. These are the things that make a difference.

The two or three things you make a priority are far more important than the little things you do all day long. These priorities are the key decisions that make the difference, not the busywork, like email. A proactive, effective CEO will look at her workload and say, "These are the three things I need to get done that will most affect my business and my life." And then she will devise processes to get those done. If you get just three important things done each day, you'll end up with about nine hundred impactful things done in a year. That's a lot of impact.

PURPOSEFUL TIME

I've found that it's relatively easy to say, "This is a priority." It's harder to move that priority to the top of your to-do list when lots of other things are pulling at your time. The key for me to prioritize anything—myself, my husband, my family, or my job—and make it stick is to make purposeful time for each priority.

The most important tasks move the work closer to long-term goals and a successful conclusion, however you've defined success. Prioritizing these tasks and activities allows me to identify the most important tasks at any moment and give those tasks more of my attention, energy, and time. It allows me to spend more time on the right things.

I tend to organize my day by impact. I obviously can't change deadlines, so those are always going to be front and center. But otherwise, I look at what's going to have the most impact for our clients, and then I focus on those things first.

I've heard that you should focus on the biggest project first, the one you dislike the most, or the one most likely to affect your success and get those out of the way. But for me, it works better if I look at what is worrying our clients the most. If I take care of that, even it's a small thing, an exponential amount of time is freed up to focus on other priorities, because I don't have the client calling or otherwise contacting me about this one, minor thing all day long. So, clients get prioritized during the workday.

I'll save my writing, thinking, and other things that need my uninterrupted attention for plane rides or weekends, because that's the only time I can really guarantee that I won't be interrupted.

To make sure I give my personal life the same priority as my work life, I give my personal appointments the same importance as my business appointments. At the beginning of each month, I reserve time for exercise, acupuncture, mentoring, and any other self-help activities I have the same way I would an appointment with a new client. I exercise just about every day, and it's just as important to me as meetings with clients, lawyers, and colleagues. It pops up on my appointment screen, and I go. If it's scheduled, it will happen.

As with anything, there are trade-offs to be made. If I'm using normal business hours for personal priorities, I often need to make up that time outside the standard Monday-to-Friday nine-to-five schedule. If have to do a couple of hours of work on a Saturday so I can do my Pilates twice a week during the day, that's worth it.

This description of my prioritization process makes it seem more straightforward than it is. This past month is a perfect example. On the last Sunday of the month, I grabbed a glass of wine and my laptop and went up to the rooftop patio to map out the next month. I've really been trying to finish a draft for an upcoming TED Talk but have not been able to get to it. I needed to find time this month, for sure. First, I added my exercise times to the calendar. Then I went back and added other standing appointments, such as my acupuncture or business coach. So far, so good. Still lots of white space in those calendar blocks. Next, I add in nonnegotiable personal and business events. Best friend's wedding will take an entire weekend. Two client events will take the better part of two days and evenings. Standing staff meetings as well as meetings with the accountant and other back-office people have populated the calendar automatically, but I check to make sure everything is there. Things are still looking good. I will definitely get to the TED Talk this month.

I see that we're interviewing for a new staff position. I'll need to make sure I'm available for those interviews. I also see that several teleconferences with clients are on the agenda. I try to set these calls for forty-five minutes so that I have fifteen minutes of cushion. I hate to be late for meetings and calls, so I always leave some time in between. If I'm lucky, I can use that time to grab a quick bite to eat or go to the bathroom.

I block out some time at the beginning of each day to return phone calls and emails on noncritical but nagging issues. While I try to prioritize activities that have the most impact on the company, I've found if I just spend a little time at the beginning of the day taking care of a bunch of little things, it gives me exponentially more time later on to focus on big things.

I keep adding things to the calendar, but now I'm beginning to look for a blank space. If it's on the calendar, I might still need to cancel, but chances are it will get done. If it's not on the calendar, it definitely won't get done.

But in general, it looks like the month will go pretty smoothly. Each day has a couple of open times for those things that inevitably pop up. All good. TED Talk, here I come.

Then I get a text. One of my staff members says they just heard from the producers of a show filmed in Hollywood who are asking me to come out this month to present a check for $10,000 to one of the charities we are supporting. We had committed to donating the money no matter what, but the show's producer heard about it from someone who knew someone and thought it would make a great addition to a segment they were doing on helping homeless women prepare for jobs. It is a good opportunity to promote EvolveMKD plus a good cause that I'd also like to promote, so I tell my assistant to accept the invitation.

If I'm going to be in California, I might as well go for the whole week and take the opportunity to see prospective clients. We had been having Skype conversations, but nothing beats face-to-face meetings. That means I need to delete the exercise times, staff meetings, back-office meetings, planning meetings, and everything else that week. In fact, once I begin listing whom I wanted to meet with, it becomes obvious that I'll need two weeks. Start canceling another week of calendar entries. When I'm traveling, my entire focus is on the client. I'll still find time to hit the hotel gym, but it's more catch as catch can. I'll need to double up on some of those canceled meetings when I get back.

And all this is before the month even starts. Other emergencies and disruptions will definitely occur that will require me to rejigger my expertly planned calendar. As I move things around, I'll keep my eye on the priorities—things that make me a better CEO and things that impact the business. Other things will just have to wait their turn. Sorry, TED Talk. You're a priority, but not a crucial priority. I'll get back to you next month.

CHALLENGE **ACCEPTED**

Client: One-of-a-kind FDA-approved aesthetic hand product.

Challenge: Launch new product line.

What EvolveMKD did: Kicking off after news of the FDA approval, a satellite media tour surrounding the Emmy Awards and video news release highlighted fall fashion trends and put a spotlight on younger-looking hands as one's best fashion accessory. A media event incorporating interactive hand-related activities, from manicures to palm readings, further emphasized the importance of caring for hands; key physicians were invited to educate attendees on the client's procedure and benefits. Inserted the brand into lifestyle and beauty content by partnering with a celebrity manicurist, who performed deskside manicures with top-tier media.

Result: Immediate coverage, including Allure.com, WomensHealth .com, Bloomberg, NewBeauty.com, and a segment on *The View*. News of the approval garnered high-impact media across print, broadcast, digital, and trade media with over 750 million total impressions.

BALANCING ACT

Prioritizing helps me keep some balance in my life, but I don't think balance has the same definition for everyone. I think my life is very balanced because I get to do everything I want to do. Yes, I spend an inordinate amount of time working and traveling for work. But I really like my job, so it doesn't seem onerous to me. And I get to see my family and friends. I spend time with my husband. But some people would look at my life and by their definition think I'm incredibly unbalanced. By my definition, I've prioritized my life in order of importance with lots of overlapping categories, and it all works.

One of the things I haven't mentioned is philanthropy. Life isn't balanced if we aren't using some of our wealth and good fortune to help others. Outreach is built into EvolveMKD's DNA. In fact, it's so important that I'm devoting the entire next chapter to it. This is the stuff that makes owning my own company worth every minute I put into it.

CHAPTER 7
COME FROM A PLACE OF #ABUNDANCE

A s the owner of a fast-growing company, it's easy to lose perspective and see only the things you need to do to improve your company, your team, or yourself. Failures, mistakes, and bumps in the road all seem to be highlighted with bright-red flashing lights, grabbing and holding everyone's attention. Conversely, things that go well seem to just fade into the background or pass by in a blur while you're distracted by those flashing warning lights.

It's not hard to understand why this happens. When our ancestors were roaming through the forest, it was a lot more important that they keep the lions at bay than notice that the trees looked particularly verdant that day. Those who stopped to smell the flowers were likely to get eaten.

It's that hypervigilance against disaster that can blot out everything else and sometimes make me wonder why I ever thought founding and growing my own company was such a good idea.

A recent week is a case in point. If something could go wrong, it did.

It started with a call from a photo/video shoot. One of our highest-profile celebrity endorsers/influencers was a no-show. Although the ad agency was in charge of the shoot, EvolveMKD was responsible for the celebrity because we had signed her as part of our campaign. This particular celebrity has a very dramatic and active social media presence, but she is actually a hardworking, extremely professional businesswoman. I have never known her to blow off a contractual commitment. A quick scan of celebrity gossip sites revealed that she had been spotted in a heated discussion with her reported love interest the night before. Was this the reason she hadn't shown up on time for the scheduled shoot or simply a piece of celebrity gossip that had no bearing on the current situation? If it was relevant, what did that really mean? Was she just late, or was she not showing up at all? No one could reach the celebrity, her assistant, or her agent. The ad agency wanted me to make a decision: Do we continue to wait and pay the assembled crew and the agency representatives to stand around doing nothing? Or do we cancel today's shoot (and eat the minimums and penalty fees associated with that) and reschedule when we find out what is happening? We decided to cancel and move on. We would have to deal with the endorser and decide what to do when we could reach her—there were penalty clauses in her contract, but did we really want to enforce those? The repercussions of this one event would follow me all week as we worked through the logistics of rescheduling the celebrity, the ad agency, our client, and my team.

But this was just the beginning. About midweek, one of our long-term clients informed me that they were going to move onto another agency. They weren't unhappy with our work, they just thought it was time for a change. This isn't unusual in our industry. Clients often think that after three or four highly creative campaigns, you have used up all your creativity and, even though they've been deliriously happy with what you've been doing, decide to move on before things begin to go downhill. It's like choosing B on HQ Trivia when there is no reason to believe B is the right answer, but as it hasn't been used for a while, it must be the answer this time. Trying to talk a client out of following their gut is a fool's errand, so we parted amicably, with me assuring them that they were always welcome back, taking the high road with wishes for much success with their new agency (though knowing I wouldn't feel too bad if things didn't work out). I then hung up the phone and resisted the urge to cry. I was frustrated, angry, and personally hurt. We had given this client our best—and they agreed that the work had been outstanding. But they were still leaving in their quest for equally outstanding work elsewhere because they just didn't think we could keep it up. How do you combat that type of reasoning? This was a personal blow to the midsection, and it took me a while to pull myself together. I take these things person- ally because EvolveMKD is me. If the former client didn't believe the company could continue to turn out the types of campaigns they had become accustomed to, then it meant that they didn't have confidence in my leadership or the team I had assembled. That's hard to take. And of course, the details of how to handle the falloff in revenues had to be dealt with. But those things are a lot easier for me to handle than someone doubting my team's abilities.

While I was still digesting the loss of the client, one of my original team members told me she was leaving. Her husband had gotten a great opportunity across the country, and they'd decided to take it. I was beginning to feel myself being sucked into the "Why me?" whirlpool. This was one of my longest-term employees. I was going to miss her. And again, it almost felt personal, though I know it wasn't.

Finally, as if the week weren't already bad enough, my accountant let me know that the new tax laws would have a negative impact on our bottom line, and he was going to have to bill extra hours looking for ways to mitigate that impact. Even Congress was against me!

So, what to do?

As public relations people, we are instinctively thinking of the worst-case scenario. It's our job to keep our clients away from those. But we can get mired in the bad stuff and think that's all there is rather than taking the time to remember the good stuff. So, after that week, I needed to reframe the narrative. That was indeed a no-good, very bad week. As I said in the beginning of this chapter, it's way too easy to focus on the things that need improvement and overlook the things that are going well. But when I took a deep breath and metaphorically took a step outside my body so I could look at the week from a distance, it was easy to see that declaring, "Anything that could go wrong, did," was a major exaggeration. Some things did indeed go wrong. But many more things went right.

Multiple studies—and many self-help gurus—have long suggested that having a positive attitude can change a situation. And it's not just that it changes the perception—it actually changes the situation.

For example, a study done by Johns Hopkins researchers called "The Power of Positive Thinking" found that those with a family history of heart disease could significantly reduce their chances of having a heart attack if they had an optimistic, positive personality.[4]

How exactly being optimistic affects health isn't known—researchers are optimistic they'll figure it out—but it might be that people who are more positive are protecting themselves against the inflammatory

---

4 "The Power of Positive Thinking," Johns Hopkins Medicine, accessed September 30, 2019, https://www.hopkinsmedicine.org/health/healthy_aging/healthy_mind/the-power-of-positive-thinking.

damage of stress, because they simply aren't feeling all that stressed. (And in the agency world, we need all the protection from stress we can get!) Another possibility is that having an optimistic outlook helps people make better health and life decisions and focus more on long-term goals.

Additional studies have found that a positive attitude improves outcomes and life satisfaction across a spectrum of conditions—including traumatic brain injury, stroke, and brain tumors.[5]

These positive health findings carry over into business. When you look at your business expecting good things, those good things seem to manifest. There's always something to be grateful for. I call it coming from a place of abundance. When I lose a client, I can moan and groan and get paralyzed from frustration and fear, or I can be thankful I had that client for as many years as I did. I can look back on everything I learned from that client and be grateful I can take those lessons and apply them to our current and future clients.

When I face a breakdown in communications, such as the one with our celebrity endorser, I can rant and rave about entitled celebrities, or I can cut her some slack and remember we all have lives that sometimes get messy. I can assume the best instead of the worst and believe she would have made the photo shoot if she could have.

My team member who is moving across country? This is an adventure she couldn't pass up. I want to run a company full of people with an insatiable curiosity and sense of adventure. That means that sometimes they will take off to follow their dream—which might also be their husband.

And the tax accounting changes? Okay, sometimes you really have to dig deep to find that place of abundance, but I can be happy that EvolveMKD is profitable and growing. We only have a tax conundrum

5   Ibid.

111

because we are growing faster than I ever projected. I really shouldn't begrudge a few more tax dollars.

This reframing technique has helped me through more than one challenge. But I've also learned that sometimes you really do have to fake it until you make it. In those cases, I just smile, say the right things, and carry on. Even if you're smiling through gritted teeth, a University of Kansas study[6] found that smiling—even fake smiling—reduces heart rate and blood pressure during stressful situations. Feeling calmer allows you to make better decisions, and better decisions soon get things back on track.

Coming from a place of abundance also affects how you treat your staff. If your default is to look for the good that people do and to assume that intentions are good, then you are going to end up supporting and praising your team a lot more than criticizing them.

Praise creates an atmosphere in which people want to work hard and do their best because they know you are recognizing them.

Your employees will pick up on that attitude and will approach their work with a positive rather than a negative attitude, which will in turn spread to the customers they engage with. Praise creates an atmosphere in which people want to work hard and do their best because they know you are recognizing them. They want to work for you (see how I brought that back around to how I take my work personally?).

One of my favorite quotes on leadership comes from Harold "Hal" Geneen, former president of ITT Corp. He stated, "Leadership

---

6   T. L. Kraft and S. D. Pressman, "Grin and bear it: the influence of manipulated facial expression on the stress response"; https://www.ncbi.nlm.nih.gov/pubmed/23012270.

is practiced not so much in words as in attitude and in actions." I try to live that by treating my team and my clients as part of the abundance of good things that surrounds me.

It's easy when you're dealing with clients to get wrapped up in their latest crisis. Taking time to step back and appreciate the success we've had as a team is important.

CHALLENGE **ACCEPTED**

Client: Medical device firm.

Challenge: Announce new process as the only minimally invasive FDA-cleared procedure in its industry.

What EvolveMKD did: Hosted multiple press trips and local market events, including in Los Angeles, Miami, and New York City, with physician meet and greets and customized wardrobe-styling sessions to showcase the treatment's lifestyle angle and benefits. Celebrated the three-year FDA clearance for the process with an interactive cocktail party, where a magical genie granted media and influencers three wishes to honor the news. Also enlisted a physician to conduct one-on-one deskside meetings with long-lead beauty and lifestyle publications to reinforce the brand credentials. Created a steady drumbeat of feature media coverage and engaging social media content with an emphasis on personal milestones and seasonal events and coordinated treatments for top-tier media and influencers to capture firsthand testimonials.

Result: Secured over 8 awards since launch, including the *Allure* Best of Beauty award, the *Good Housekeeping* Beauty Break-through Award, and the *RealSelf* Most Worth It Award. Earned over 2 billion traditional media impressions since launch and nearly 100 million social media impressions across Facebook, Twitter, Instagram, Pinterest, and YouTube. Was Marcom's Gold Award Winner in the Social Media Campaign and Social Media Content categories.

LOOKING FOR THE GOOD

Each one of our clients plays a part in surrounding us with abundance, and so I always try to make sure they feel that we are laser focused on their needs. The clients that come to us—whether it's a business they've started, or they are part of a larger company—take pride in what they do. They care. I am very cognizant that companies these days have limited marketing / advertising / public relations budgets, so if they've decided to invest in us, that's a pretty big decision. From our perspective, we take it personally, in a good way. We recognize and are grateful for the investment in us and our team. We are especially thankful for our early clients, who took a risk by coming with us before we were a known entity. We take that badge of confidence and trust really seriously.

That's also part of why the team members care so much when they're working on clients and why we are so selective when we take clients. There is an emotional investment as well is a mental and work investment. It's like dating. You want to be selective with whom you spend your time.

This selectivity extends to hiring team members as well. While I can set the example and hope the team will play nicely in the sandbox I provide, I try to hire people who have an optimistic outlook from the beginning. Sussing out these soft personality aspects is difficult. I can look at past work and talk to them about their skill sets. That's easy. But how do you determine if someone looks at the world from a place of abundance or sees it as a zero-sum game where you have to ruthlessly grab yours or someone else will?

One of the questions I like to ask in an interview is "What drives you? Do you love to win or hate to lose?" Think about how you'd answer that. Picture how you've reacted to winning and losing. Do you have a greater emotional response when you win or when you lose? In my experience, those who hate to lose typically care much more about their work than those who love to win. The "love to win" crowd tends to be really happy when they win but just meh when they lose. The "hate to lose" contingent, on the other hand, will work much harder to avoid losing than the "love to win" crowd, who prefer to win but aren't that upset if they lose. I tend to gravitate toward the "hate to lose" applicant, because I think he or she will care more and go above and beyond to make sure the client's needs are taken care of. Of course, I could just be justifying my own intense dislike of losing. Some might even call me a sore loser, though I prefer to think of it as a totally appropriate reaction to disappointing myself or my team.

Despite my preference for "hate to lose" teammates, the characteristics I think make a really good Evolver are hard to get from a thirty-minute interview. I want people who have learned that self-awareness is really important and have a healthy mental outlook and a healthy way of taking care of themselves. But you can't just ask if they are self-aware. I suppose if I asked that and they responded, "I don't know," then I would have my answer, but we all know it goes deeper than that. We have high standards, and we know what works, but the things that make someone a really good teammate are hard to pinpoint until you start working with the person.

So far, I've been very lucky in that nearly all the people we've hired have not only fit well into our culture but have enhanced it. I think this proves the point that if you treat people with generosity and respect, they will reflect those qualities back to you. And it becomes a virtuous circle that perpetuates a culture of abundance.

MAKE PHILANTHROPY A PRIORITY

When I talk about coming from a place of abundance, I also include philanthropic initiatives. Saying that you are surrounded by abundance rings pretty hollow if you aren't willing to share some of it.

> *Saying that you are surrounded by abundance rings pretty hollow if you aren't willing to share some of it.*

I've said often through this book that I wanted EvolveMKD to be different from other agencies I'd worked for. I wanted it to be a place that reflected how I think people should be treated, whether they are team members, vendors, or clients. But I also wanted it to be a living, breathing part of the community. Too often, people walk by a building and never know what is behind the facade. I wanted people in the community to know that EvolveMKD is behind that facade—and that we are part of the fabric of the life that goes on in our neighborhood.

I believe successful business owners have a responsibility to the community around them to create and give opportunities to everyone. This responsibility is just part of being a good corporate citizen. However, a company that sees itself as rooted in its community not only helps those around it but attracts high-quality people who want to be part of a socially conscious and ethical company. You would hope that they would have oodles of companies to choose from. Unfortunately, that is not the case.

We have made giving a part of the EvolveMKD culture by involving the entire team in the projects we donate time, energy, and money to. Socially conscious initiatives need to start at and be supported by the top, and the entire team needs to feel a part of it if it is to become a self-sustaining core value. To ensure that everyone on the team knows that their involvement is crucial—and we are not just paying lip service to the notion that the team is involved—we primarily focus our donations on causes suggested by staff.

Being an ethical company, where giving is just a given, is at the core of who I am. I simply couldn't run a company in any other way. However, in addition to making me feel good, making my team members feel good, and hopefully making the people we help feel good, several studies have shown that companies that do good also do well. In fact, they do better—that is, are more profitable—than those focused on holding on to every penny of revenue for their owners and shareholders. Having socially conscious strategies is not just good public relations; it's good business.

In their book *Firms of Endearment: How World-Class Companies Profit from Passion and Purpose,* Raj Sisodia and Jag Sheth find that firms that focus on being ethical and doing good rather than just the bottom line actually outperform those with a less altruistic approach. They have found that today's greatest companies are fueled by passion and purpose, not cash. They earn large profits by helping all their stakeholders thrive—customers, investors, employees, partners, communities, and society as a whole. In fact, the firms of endearment featured in their book have outperformed the S&P 500 by fourteen times, or 1,400 percent, during a recent fifteen-year period. Before you say that a lot of those S&P 500 companies have seen better days, the authors found that the firms of endearment outperformed even those rated as good to great by six times—or 600 percent.

Other studies have found the link between altruism and profits to be more tenuous, but donating a portion of our profits and some of our time isn't based on enhancing revenues. It's great to know that at least in some studies, generous companies are more successful than those who focus only on shareholder value—and I plan to be one of those more successful companies—but that's not why I make giving a priority. This goes back to my contention that good business is always personal. My business is a reflection of who I am. It needs to reflect my core values. I don't believe that any business can be truly successful if it is run in a value-free vacuum. So, as part of my values, I believe that successful business owners have a responsibility to the community to give everyone the opportunity to be successful. And we have made that responsibility part of EvolveMKD's DNA.

To effectively weave philanthropy into a company's culture, you need to have people actively participate. Donating money to a good cause is certainly laudable—and we do that—but you want people to be personally involved. To encourage that participation, we make sure we are supporting causes the team members feel strongly about. So far, these have primarily involved organizations or events that benefit women and children. We can see the need these organizations are meeting, and it is a strong incentive to continue to help.

We also make sure our goals are manageable. I would love to do a service day a month, but that's not realistic. Sometimes I don't get to see my husband that much in a month! Once a quarter is much more manageable (to do a service day, not see my husband). So, our goal is to have an optional service day once a quarter. No one is required to participate, but nearly everyone does. And the reason nearly everyone does is because we not only make it easy for them to do so by taking care of all the logistics, but as I mentioned earlier, we choose causes that our people care about. A lot of these causes are very local, which means EvolveMKD is seen as an integral part of the community, and the team members get to see the results of their giving. Keeping it local, working with the people who need your help, seeing the results—all are super motivating factors that keep the team coming back time and again.

You also have to acknowledge that these are goals, not requirements, and not beat yourself up if you fall short at times. For some reason, first quarter is always crazy for us, and second quarter is a little bit less crazy, although every year has been different. So, last year we didn't do a service day in the first quarter, but we did two in the second. We allow ourselves the flexibility to go with the flow a little bit and not overwhelm ourselves.

A major part of encouraging a culture of giving and coming from a place of abundance is to have the corporation itself involved. While we all personally give our time, EvolveMKD donates 10 percent of its profits to causes selected by the team. To ensure we really are hitting our 10 percent target, I aggressively track it each month. Obviously, profits can fluctuate per month, but at the end of the year, I make sure that overall, we have truly hit 10 percent. Philanthropy isn't an afterthought or a "nice to do" thing at EvolveMKD. It's a priority, and we make it front and center when we are doing our end-of-the-year financial consolidations.

I mentioned that we look for causes that the team feels strongly about. In doing so, we often look at organizations and activities that also have some sort of aesthetic tie. This makes a lot of sense, given our client base and the interests of the team. For example, we've worked with domestic abuse survivor organizations, which provide support for women who need help feeling empowered as well as safe. A lot of this support involves making these women look and feel good. We know how to help with that. We've donated to Look Good, Feel Better, which is a program for women who are emerging from cancer treatment. We make sure they know the best products to use for skin care and how to do their hair. We also are wide open to suggestions from the team. For example, the best friend of one of our staffers passed away from cystic fibrosis last year, so we made a big donation to the Cystic Fibrosis Foundation in her honor. We've also donated to the ASPCA and to Junior League charitable events at the suggestion of team members.

The public relations and digital marketing business is hard. You are at your clients' beck and call, and things can go wrong very quickly. But knowing you are supported by a company that recognizes the needs of its staff makes it easier to put in the hours and handle the stress. The team is always excited when a service day rolls around. I know it's one of the things that make working at EvolveMKD different and one of the things they really appreciate. I think we could probably do a better job promoting it when we are recruiting new hires, but that always feels weird to me. We aren't doing it to recruit better team members. I'm aware of the irony. If I were my own client, I would tell us that we have to promote it more. But working hard, being responsible, being grateful, and sharing the wealth is just part of who we are. It's not part of a campaign. And so far, just being who we are works for us.

CHALLENGE **ACCEPTED**

Client: International skin care firm.

Challenge: Launch celebrity endorser as the global brand ambassador for the natural skin care line while also differentiating the brand from other natural skin care offerings available at mass retail.

What EvolveMKD did: Kicked off the partnership announcement with a post on the celebrity's social media channels featuring an exclusive photo from her skin care campaign shoot followed by press release distribution and national media outreach. Coordinated New York City and Los Angeles media days to provide top-tier media, including Allure.com, *WWD,* and Byrdie.com, the opportunity to engage with the celebrity in one-on-one interviews and hosted cocktail parties for additional media and influencers to take photo-booth selfies with the celebrity endorser for instant social media posts. Partnered with Amazon to capture video content featuring the endorser and her favorite products to drive viewers to Amazon.com for purchase.

Result: Within 24 hours of the official announcement, secured over 232 million media impressions in national outlets. Coordinated exclusive feature coverage of the partnership with the *TODAY* show and *People* as well as global broadcast segments with the UK's *This Morning* and Australia's *Today Extra.* Engaged over 80 key media and influencers through media days hosted in New York City and Los Angeles.

CHAPTER 8
#LIFE HAPPENS

No one would ever accuse me of being laid back and laissez faire. I'm a driven, take-no-prisoners person. The ability to plan, focus, execute, and just keep going until it's done are traits that have served me well, both in life and business. But sometimes the best-laid plans get blindsided by forces beyond your control. Life happens. And you better be able to change course and go with it, or you're likely to be permanently derailed.

I have a client who got married a few years ago in Oregon. She, too, is a planner. She chose the venue years in advance—well before she had even met her fiancé. She just knew that when her wedding day arrived, she wanted to say her vows under a canopy of trees in the hills of Oregon. The more than two hundred guests would then enjoy a gourmet meal catered by the best caterers in Portland and dance the night away under the stars. She even chose the date based on the phase of the moon (full moons are beautiful, but stars shine brighter in other phases) and the historical likelihood of having a clear night.

Her envisioned perfect wedding always reminded me of the poem "The Owl and the Pussy-Cat," where "they danced by the light of the moon, the moon, the moon."

Then the wildfires started.

Two days before her planned-to-the-most-finite-detail wedding, the hills around her town were a raging inferno. By the time it all ended—weeks after the wedding—those fires would burn a record number of Oregon acres. A large number of populated areas were being evacuated. Even larger areas were being pelted by falling soot and surrounded by a deep haze of choking fog. Her dream wedding was literally going up in smoke.

Never one to stand still, she quickly changed course. A dream is just a dream. Reality is what we live in. The wedding would go on— just differently. The only large venue available—nearly anything not in the evacuation area was booked—was a generic hotel conference center twenty-five miles away. Not exactly her tree canopy, but she grabbed it. She contacted the caterers about reducing the number of meals (many of her guests would not be able to make it because travel was restricted or they were focused on their own situation, like finding temporary housing). It turned out it was too late to change the catering order, so she decided to just accept all the meals originally ordered but have half of them delivered boxed so she could take them to a local fire station after the wedding. She sent emails and texts to as many guests as she could to give them the new details, but she went the extra mile to make sure her guests knew the wedding was still on. She contacted local news stations with her story. She knew it was exactly the type of human interest story that news directors lust for when covering huge natural disasters like out-of-control wildfires. She was covered by all the local stations and picked up by a couple of the national networks. Anyone invited was assured the show would go on.

The day of the wedding came, as it was going to do no matter what. Those who could make it did, and those who couldn't didn't. My client had found a quick-print company that was able to print the bride's and groom's initials and wedding date on dust masks, which were handed out to everyone as favors. Dancing to a Spotify list took the place of a live band. Instead of stars twinkling overhead, the sound of helicopters could be heard, and the orange glow of flames in the surrounding hills reflected off the mirrored walls.

Nothing was as planned. But you know what? The two were just as married at the end of this event as they would have been if their original plans had panned out. Which is the whole idea of a wedding, isn't it?

Everyone had a blast. And everyone went away with a story about love conquering all. It was certainly a wedding to remember.

As EvolveMKD has grown, I've found it more important than ever to remember that life can be messy. No matter what the level of intensity is in your business at the moment, life is still happening around you. It's important not to miss it, and it's important to give those moments in life their fair due. And it's also important to remember that tomorrow will come no matter what is happening today, and life will go on.

CHALLENGE **ACCEPTED**

Client: Aesthetic medical device firm.

Challenge: Increase brand awareness and sales of the firm's in-office aesthetic systems via a world tour.

What EvolveMKD did: Distributed a press release that introduced the world tour campaign and worked with providers to ensure that media and influencers who could not attend the tour got to experience a sample treatment. Coordinated tour stops in all major key markets, including New York City, Boston, Chicago, Denver, Philadelphia, San Francisco, Los Angeles, and more, where media and influencers were treated to the firm's aesthetic processes. Arranged "stops" at publishing houses, where the firm's practitioners spent a day at Conde Nast, Hearst, and PopSugar, and provided each editor and writer with a personalized facial.

Result: A feature segment on *Good Morning America* and giveaway on the *TODAY* show. National media coverage in outlets including *Vogue*, *Allure*, *Glamour*, and *InTouch*, exceeding the one-billion-impressions goal for the tour. Each stop resulted in the sale of five or more facial systems.

LIFE AND EMPLOYEES

The culture of EvolveMKD revolves around respect—respect for the clients, respect for our work, and respect for each other. We work as a team to deliver outstanding results for our clients but also to support each other. So, if someone needs to be out, the others just pick up the slack. No one feels they are being taken advantage of. They know that if they need time away, the others will have their back as well.

We had a team member last year whose best friend was hospitalized and unfortunately ended up passing away. She was only thirty, and it hit everyone hard. That team member was in and out for six weeks, dealing with the whole thing. And we supported her taking all the time she needed. Let's face it—your best friend passing away is definitely way more important than any work we've got going on.

Too many companies claim they put people first and promote work-life balance but then give their employees only three days of bereavement leave—and the person who is being mourned typically has to be a first-degree relative, such as a parent, sibling, or child. A best friend wouldn't count. A grandparent or an uncle might not even count. This type of policy is not what I'd consider employee friendly or putting people first.

When my team member was grieving her friend, I set the tone for others at EvolveMKD. I made it very clear that the team member not only was *free* to take as much time as she needed but was *encouraged* to take that time. The team just banded together to help her. Because I take business personally, my team does too. This was not just a casual colleague who needed support. She was a friend and an integral part of the team. When you allow your team members to feel a sense of ownership in the company, they will step up every time. EvolveMKD is their company as well as mine. This was their teammate. And they would help in any way they could. And they all know they can count on the company to stand behind them as well if life interferes.

Showing your team members that you see them as unique people with all the wants, needs, and quirks that come with that will engender loyalty and a desire to give their best.

While I support my staff just because it's the right thing to do, having a corporate culture that recognizes that we all have lives outside of work enhances the job done inside of work. Showing your team members that you see them as unique people with all the wants, needs, and quirks that come with that will engender loyalty and a desire to give their best. They know they can focus on their work most of the time because you are allowing them to take care of their personal lives as well when needed.

Most traditional public relations and social media agencies have what I call a burnout culture. You bring young people in. You drive them for twenty hours a day. You get the best out of them. You burn them out. You cast them off. You get the next group in. Repeat. Frankly, this model has a fair number of pros to go with the cons. If it weren't useful, it wouldn't be so deeply ingrained in the industry.

From a management viewpoint, for example, the burnout model is easier, because you just churn and burn. You don't have to worry about the culture. You don't have to worry about spending a lot of effort customizing benefits. You don't have to worry how people get along. It doesn't matter. So, as a business owner, it's easier to staff your business that way.

But I don't think that's the right way to do it. My way is a lot more work, and it definitely causes me a lot more heartache, because no matter what you do, you can't make everyone happy. But treating people with respect has long-term benefits you don't get from the traditional model. For example, I've had several senior and midlevel staff with me since the beginning (or close to the beginning) of the business. These are people who have chosen to work at EvolveMKD precisely because we treat them like responsible adults and provide the compensation packages their skills merit. Having this consistency is a huge bonus when it comes to the trust our clients have in us. The clients who have been with us from the beginning know the people on the team as well as they know me. You can't overestimate how important this trust and continuing long-term relationships are when things get a bit bumpy. I'm sure there were times when we were in danger of losing clients, but the relationship they had with the team kept them on board long enough for us to make things right and provide the next outstanding campaign.

These senior people recognize that providing flexibility is a lot of work and that I don't have to do it that way. They appreciate it, and they stay. We're a little more top heavy than most agencies, but I purposely hire people who've already worked one or two other places and have a track record, so they're a bit more educated about the choice they're making in terms of employment. I know I expect a lot. But then I also feel like I give a lot. And I think that's the difference.

Every agency expects a lot because clients expect a lot. But employees often don't get a lot for giving a lot. I know there are things we could do to improve, but I think the fact that we have a top-tier benefits and compensation package plus the fact that I'm so flexible is very unusual. And the loyalty of my staff proves that it's well worth it.

Providing this type of flexibility within a company doesn't just randomly happen. First of all, I hire people who I know are responsible adults who won't take advantage of our flexibility. I also hire the type of people who don't look for reasons to be aggrieved. I want people who know that we're going to do our best to make things fair. We're really going try to do the right thing by everyone, but that might come in different packages. Being fair doesn't mean doing everything the same. It means being equitable.

I'm not a big believer in the concept of one size fits all. I know it is going get harder to provide flexible benefits as we get bigger, but I'm very committed to it. I don't think there's one benefit, one policy, or one anything that everyone is going use the same way. For example, a standard maternity leave is twelve weeks. Taking that amount of time off simply doesn't sound appealing to me. So, while I'd be grateful for the option to take three months off, I can imagine my maternity leave being much shorter. Some women might want to take even longer off. In Europe, we know a typical leave stretches a year or more. Or other women might want some combination of being totally off for a few weeks, then working part time from home, then maybe back full time with some flexibility to work from home some of the time. I just feel like it's part of being a good business owner to work with all employees to give them the flexibility and customization they need—assuming the person is a good performer and is a team player themselves—because everyone's life is not the same.

Not too long ago, one of my longtime team members came back from her twelve weeks of maternity leave. She is an awesome worker, so we were all looking forward to getting her back on projects. But it soon became obvious that things had changed. Her heart wasn't in it anymore. She desperately wanted to be home, but for financial reasons, she had to work. A lot of companies would have let her go. Agency life is very much a "What have you done for me lately?" type of business, and the policies are based on what is best for the business. But that's not how I would want to be treated, and so it's not how I treat my team. I called her in and laid out every option I could think of that would allow her to keep working. I was looking for options that were best for her, not what was best for me. At the end of the meeting, I told her, "Look, here are all the options and the pros and cons of each. You tell me what works for you, and I will make it work."

I know that her needs will change over time. In a few months, she might not need so much time at home, and then we'll revisit our options. In the meantime, I have an experienced professional continuing to turn out high-quality work and making clients ever so glad they chose EvolveMKD as their agency. And I have a person who will remember that we went the extra mile for her when she needed it, and she will likely go the extra mile for us in return if we need it.

That seems like a win-win situation to me.

The focus of flexible work situations is often on women (and more often now, men) with children, but that's not fair to other employees. I might want to leave early to meet with friends whom I haven't seen in a while. That should carry just as much weight as people leaving to pick up their children at day care. Someday, I'd like to be able to offer sabbaticals to all my workers who have been here for a specific amount of time, because it's not right that you have to be pregnant to get several months off. As a country, we seem to have an obsession about how we help working moms and dads balance it all, and I think that's really important. But I also think a lot of people don't choose that path. And they also deserve flexibility. It just needs to be fair, no matter what your life choice is.

LIFE AND CLIENTS

Of course, we need to balance the needs of clients with the needs of staff. We are, after all, a business. Work is important. That's sort of the definition of a company, isn't it? And certainly all our clients are important. But sometimes things do happen that are more important than an individual deadline.

The primary way I balance the needs of everyone is to try to head off conflicts before they occur. This starts with the hiring process. If I hire people who are responsible and don't take advantage of the flexibility we give them to live their lives, we will rarely have a situation in which a client feels shortchanged.

In the same vein, we are very selective about whom we take on as a client. We do not take on jerks. A lot of companies are used to dealing with agencies that use the churn-and-burn model. They might be dealing with a different account exec every six months or so. As such, they never get to know their account rep on a personal basis and often treat them dismissively. They feel if the agency is disrespecting the representative, then they can do so too. I don't treat our staff that way, and I don't expect my clients to treat them that way. In fact, not only do I not expect it, I don't put up with it. Any client who abuses my staff is soon a former client.

Our client selection focuses on working with people who understand that there are humans on both sides of the phone. This goes back to the beginning of the book when I talked about only taking on clients who saw us as a real partner, not as just as someone to execute tasks. This is a two-way street. We ask that they recognize us as human beings, but we also commit to not taking advantage of our clients' good natures and flexibility.

To build the goodwill that allows a client to accept changes in timelines and deliverables when life invariably happens, you need to deliver outstanding service—in fact, overdeliver outstanding service—during the majority of the time when life is not interfering. I've talked to clients at night and on weekends. I've talked to them on the way to and from the airport and while at the gym. I don't make it a habit, because you have to have boundaries, but if you show flexibility to work around their life and you're delivering good results, they're more than happy to work around yours.

Work-life balance has become something of a buzzword. People often see work and life as two separate things divided by a bright-red line. I prefer to look at the concept more like a seesaw or maybe like the ocean ebbing and flowing. Sometimes work is going to be taking up most of your time, and sometimes life outside of work is going to be front and center. For someone like me who loves her work and is energized by the challenges, the two are completely interwoven. A company that sees its employees as real people and not just staff members on an org chart will recognize that and make every effort to accommodate individual needs. I like to think EvolveMKD is that company now and will be able to be that company no matter how large we grow. I know it will be harder to accommodate everyone as we acquire more clients and employees, but it shouldn't be impossible. A little creativity always goes a long way. And what is more creative than a public relations and digital marketing agency?

CHALLENGE **ACCEPTED**

Client: International medical device firm.

Challenge: Expose procedure to a broader consumer audience and allow the opportunity to generate an ongoing conversation among consumers.

What EvolveMKD did: Partnered with a fitness and lifestyle TV personality and online influencer, who was treated with the procedure. Offered the opportunity to promote her first-person experience. Developed a multitype content series, timed with the beginning of summer, featuring exercises that would help firm the thighs and buttocks. Content included a mix of short videos, animated stop motion, infographics, and photo galleries. Launched on the brand's social media channels supported by hypertargeted ads and also featured on partner's social media channels for added exposure among targeted female fitness-enthusiast fan base. Content leveraged popular trending days (i.e., #MotivationMonday, #WorkoutWednesday, #FitnessFriday) for organic user discovery.

Result: Delivered over 2.47 million impressions across a two-month campaign period. Generated 989,600 consumer engagements across Facebook, Instagram, Twitter, Pinterest, and YouTube. Garnered a 40 percent engagement rate on brand-owned channels and a 16 percent engagement rate on partner's channels. Named Marcom's Gold Award Winner in the Social Media Campaign and Social Media Content categories.

CHAPTER 9

TAKING #EVOLVEMKD AND OUR CLIENTS INTO THE #FUTURE

Before becoming a business owner, I used to sit at my desk at whatever agency I was working at and think about how I'd do things differently. When it was finally time for me to put my daydreams into action, I jumped in with both feet and naive enthusiasm. Turns out daydreams tend to be a bit light on details. All that mist around the edges and scenes shot through filters make the vision lovely and appealing. But the details of execution are hidden behind the screen. It was easy to say that my agency would be different. My clients would treat me as a full partner in developing their strategies. My company culture would come from a place of abundance and recognize that life happens. We would merge traditional public relations with digital and social media marketing. We'd focus on innovators and innovations that positively affect health and well-being. But what does that all mean in real terms? How do I translate those philosophies into actionable processes?

Throughout this book, I've outlined the strategies I've hit upon that have made that daydream a reality. I'm still working on fine-tuning elements of my business, but the past few years have proven that it is indeed possible to grow an unorthodox culture that puts people first without sacrificing corporate growth. But in making my dreams a reality, I've rarely looked too far into the future.

Instead, the past few years have been spent getting EvolveMKD off the ground and working around the clock to make sure it stayed that way. Now that I have a little breathing room (getting a new business off the ground is hard!), I've been looking to the future. Now that I'm confident that EvolveMKD will still be humming along for many years to come, I need to articulate and plan for where I expect to be in three, five, even ten years.

KEEPING OUR IDENTITY WHILE GROWING UP

If I start by looking at how I expect the company culture to evolve, I know it will be hard to continue to offer company-paid top-tier insurance to all employees. It will be hard to continue to offer individual benefits and flexible leave policies. I know that when I have sixty employees versus the current twenty-five-plus, I'll need to formalize some of the processes. But I also know that just because something is hard, it doesn't mean it's impossible. In fact, I get excited about finding solutions to challenging problems. It gets my blood flowing and wakes up my competitive nature.

Our forecast shows continued growth, both in revenues and staff, so we have begun to prepare for the time when we will need more formalized and standardized processes to continue to function efficiently. To that end, we've already hired a chief of staff, who is helping to standardize processes while keeping the flexible and people-focused nature that is so important to EvolveMKD culture.

CHALLENGE **ACCEPTED**

Client: Biotech firm.

Challenge: Use a digital-first strategy to raise awareness of genetic testing products.

What EvolveMKD did: With a minimal audience across its consumer-facing social media channels, focused our launch efforts around acquiring a highly targeted audience and engagement within that audience set. Through a mix of paid media, compelling content, and a highly responsive fan communication system, were able to drive strong results within the first six months. With an engaged audience in place, turned our focus to website traffic and acquiring leads through focused social media clicks-to-website (CTW) web and lead-generation campaigns.

Result: Within six months, increased traffic across social media channels.

Primary channels:
- Facebook fans: +16,453 percent
- Instagram followers: +865 percent

Secondary channels:
- Pinterest followers: +150 percent
- Twitter followers: +154 percent

The campaign to drive web traffic also proved successful, with a 120 percent increase in website traffic and over a hundred new leads generated each month.

I know I need these more formalized policies, but they can still come from a place that takes the needs of the employee into account rather than just those of the business. When it comes to our philanthropy, I always expect to donate at least 10 percent of our profits, but as we grow, instead of donating to various charities suggested by staff members, I can see us setting up a foundation with charitable guidelines so that there is more logic and consistency to where the money is going. Instead of being completely flexible on leaves and other policies, I can see setting up more formal policies that could still be adjusted on a case-by-case basis if needed. Whatever I do, it will continue to be within the framework of our current culture, which makes business personal and puts people above profits.

Looking at EvolveMKD from a macro level, I think what we have created is the future of small business. At least, I hope it is. Imagine if all small businesses adopted the EvolveMKD mindset. How much would the lives of millions of people be changed if all businesses truly focused on the needs of their staff with measurable, observable employee-friendly policies such as flexible leave and high-tier company-paid insurance?

And don't let the "small business" moniker fool you into thinking these firms wouldn't have that much of an impact. Small businesses are the backbone of the US economic system and have a huge impact on business mores and practices.

According to the Small Business Administration, small businesses make up 99.9 percent of all US firms. And before you say, "Sure, but a lot of those firms are sole proprietorships," stats also show that 99.7 percent of firms with paid employees fall into the small business category. Nearly 48 percent of private employees (58 million out of 121 million employees) work in small businesses. Small businesses also drive growth, accounting for 61.8 percent of net new jobs from the first quarter of 1993 until the third quarter of 2016.[7]

Small businesses are always at risk of failing from lack of cash flow because they don't have the resources of huge public corporations. As such, employee benefits obviously need to be balanced with the need of the business to survive, but too often we concentrate on bottom-line numbers and don't even try to find ways to provide more for employees while continuing to grow the business. A little creativity and flexibility goes a long way to finding the right balance.

PUBLIC RELATIONS AND SOCIAL MEDIA IN THE SPOTLIGHT

Moving to a more micro level, public relations and social media are evolving into an integral part of every business. It's not just spinning or crisis management; it's controlling your own narrative and destiny. Every business needs to do that. A lot of people talk about the changing world of public relations and reputation management, but the core of the industry has been the same for decades and will probably remain the same for decades to come. Briefly, it has been and still is the job of public relations professionals to protect and enhance our clients' reputations and get their products in front of target audiences. What is changing—and changing dramatically—is the way we are getting the message to those audiences.

Social media is a core channel for our campaigns now, but it will be even more important as companies realize they need to reach and interact with their target markets on a more personal level than ever before. People now expect companies and brands to be things that

---

7   US Small Business Administration Office of Advocacy, "Frequently Asked Questions About Small Business" (August 2017), https://www.sba.gov/sites/default/files/advocacy/SB-FAQ-2017-WEB.pdf?utm_medium=email&utm_source=govdelivery.

they believe in, that they feel good about. Using creative campaigns on social media and other digital platforms is the best way to show audiences the inner workings of companies and let them know that these firms share their ethics and values—as well as promote their products.

Being able to embrace and stay abreast—and optimally, stay ahead—of these changes will mean the difference between surviving and not. This isn't a new concept. The Pony Express did not go out of business the day after the transcontinental telegraph system was completed on October 24, 1861, because people no longer needed to send messages. It went out of business because telegrams were a more efficient method of sending messages than saddlebags on fast horses. There was no way for the Pony Express to compete, so it went out of business. Netflix drove Blockbuster out of business. Uber and Lyft are putting pressure on traditional taxi services. Amazon is changing the face of retail. None of these corporations changed consumer needs. They simply met those needs better than the traditional model. It really is an "adapt or die" world.

If we are going to deliver successful campaigns, we need to believe in the company, not just the product.

Knowing that, EvolveMKD is adapting. In fact, with our focus on digital channels, we are in the forefront of delivering value to our clients via new and expanding channels. We are also demanding that the vendor/client relationship change. If we are going to deliver successful campaigns, we need to believe in the company, not just the product.

As a public relations professional, I help my clients shape their message so that their audience can see the company culture behind the product. What's your positioning? What are your priorities? What is your vision and mission? Historically, public relations has not been part of these strategic decisions, but if we're involved in those discussions and can help shape them, then our output is so much better. In the past, public relations agencies have just been handed things to execute. When I started EvolveMKD, we mandated from day one that we have a seat at the table for those discussions. That's our expectation, and most of our current clients respect that. Going forward, as we grow, we will only accept clients based on their willingness to allow us in the room where it happens. And we might drop a couple that don't.

But we want to do more to change the industry. We are actively working on finding better ways to measure success. There is a real need in the industry to develop better data metrics to determine ROI. The days of unlimited marketing, advertising, and public relations budgets are over. Our clients need and deserve to know that their dollars are being spent wisely. The current counting of hits and clicks just doesn't tell us enough—although we are getting better at determining why some hits translate into sales and why some don't. Becoming more data driven, both in campaign solutions and results analyses, will give the industry a credibility it does not always possess.

I envision EvolveMKD continuing to lead this evolution as we diversify and begin taking on more traditional marketing functions. As it stands, the boundaries between marketing, advertising, and public relations are already soft. Jumping a little more into the marketing side, where we can help develop brand strategy and outreach, makes a lot of sense.

We have plans to expand our digital marketing offerings and capabilities through a combination of acquisition and key talent iden-tification. We are also working on enhancing our content capabilities. It's a lot of work to provide content for blogs, vlogs, and other channels that educate the consumer as well as promote a product or client, but information is what drives consumers to our clients' websites.

We also have plans to diversify by targeted market/consumer, and we're adding sectors such as genetics and CBD-based products that are becoming more and more part of consumers' lives. That being said, I don't look at EvolveMKD as an industry-specific agency. Obviously, right now we have a huge tilt toward technological advancement with all our products. I suspect this will always be true just because those products and entrepreneurial-type companies are really interesting to me. However, what we are really looking at, regardless of industry, are best-in-class products or significant innovations or something truly new that really enhances a person's life or experience. It could be a product, service, or company as long as it is really and truly new.

A lot of people also think of us as just a female-run, female-focused firm. And that's true in a high-level way. But when you look at us at ground level, you'll see it is more nuanced. We run campaigns geared to the female purchaser. Not the female consumer—the female purchaser. Women drive 85 percent of all consumer purchasing.[8] If they aren't purchasing the product themselves, they are influencing or have veto power over someone who is. That means we will take on just about any product that fits our model, because every product is of interest to the female purchaser or influencer. As we continue to grow and take on more clients and innovative products, I'd like to make that distinction clearer.

Long term, I can see us going global via partnerships. The one thing we'll have to watch for is culture fit. I would want any firm we partner with to provide the same level of service to clients and the same respect for employees that we do. They would have to work the

---

8   "Statistics on the Purchasing Power of Women," Yankelov-
    ich Monitor / Greenfield Online, https://girlpowermarketing.com/
    statistics-purchasing-power-women/

same way we do. Very few American companies work the way we do, so finding compatible firms in Europe, Asia, and South America seems doubly difficult. But as I said before, hard doesn't mean impossible. This is a challenge I'll love to take on when the time is right.

One of the things I'm most excited about is an initiative we're working on to provide a type of scaled-down or off-the-shelf public relations product to smaller brands that aren't ready for prime time yet but still need help. I envision this as a type of incubator program, where the firms are interesting to us because of their innovative culture or product but don't have the budget for the soup-to-nuts plan. In those cases, we would come up with something that's a little bit more grassroots for them that we hand off and they implement with their own in-house staff. That way, we can keep them in the family and be there when they are ready for a larger commitment. It's a way to build a pipeline of young entrepreneurial clients rather than just picking them up one at a time after they've matured.

Through all this expansion, we'll always be focused on deepening our current client partnerships. With each added capability, sector, or service, we will be providing better and deeper personal, bespoke service to each client. We are prioritizing growth, but we won't ever lose our focus on our clients.

CHALLENGE **ACCEPTED**

Client: Aesthetic product.

Challenge: Launch new product, a game changer in its market, to top-tier health, entertainment, and beauty media.

What EvolveMKD did: Hosted a series of lunch-and-learn media events with network surgeons in top media markets to educate media and influencers, showcasing the product's innovation and unique technology. Partnered with a celebrity endorser, who dropped a competitive product in favor of the game changer, which was covered by People.com and additional top-tier entertainment media outlets.

Result: Since the launch of the campaign, over 2 billion impressions have been secured, including a segment on *The Doctors*, an article in the *New York Times*, and features in multiple long-lead magazines. The buzz was amplified with *Yahoo! Beauty* naming the product among its "7 Biggest Beauty Breakthroughs" and *Refinery29* calling it the "future of [the industry]."

EPILOGUE

#MEGAN'S RULES

MEGAN'S RULES

- Listen to the universe. If you pay attention, you can usually discern signals on what to do.

- Trust your gut. You know what has worked in the past. Don't discount that knowledge.

- Take everything personally. It *is* about you.

- Outhustle everyone else—it will pay off.

- Don't hire or work with jerks. In a culture like EvolveMKD where we offer a lot of flexibility, one person taking advantage of that flexibility can bring down the whole team.

- Be picky when taking on clients. Having no client is better than having a bad client.

- Be disciplined about balance—if you don't try for it, no one else will do it for you!

- Don't let fear stop you from something you want to do.

- Take it personally. Business decisions are personal decisions. Don't be afraid to invest them with the emotion and gravitas they deserve.

"Don't take it personally. It's just business."

How often have you heard that? Every day, I bet. It's so ingrained in our work ethic that everyone just accepts it. But it's wrong. Business should be personal.

I take business personally every day. I don't separate my business from my life, and the same rules that I've found work for living life to the fullest also apply to business. I don't know any other way to work. Which is okay, because it has allowed me to grow a company that is making waves in the public relations and social media industry and that I believe will continue to burst through the standard ways we've always run agencies.

I feel so strongly that the best way to conduct business is to make it personal that I'm doing a TED Talk on it. I haven't quite completed it yet—as I mentioned in the chapter on priorities, it isn't a crucial priority, so it keeps getting bounced—but I know what I'm going to say.

I'll start with an anecdote illustrating my aha moment, the instant I realized that the way I instinctively run my business isn't something I should change but something I should embrace. I'll then run through some examples of comparing how traditional corporate models have treated their clients and employees versus how EvolveMKD does. And then I'll get to the heart of the matter: how you conduct yourself and your business matters. Today's clients, employees, and public in general want to work with a company they believe in and that shares their values. They want to know that the company they are giving their money to or taking advice from is ethical and focused on making life better for its customers, employees, and the community in general. Social media has changed how we view the world. We want to see the face behind the message. We want to see the humans behind the product.

Humanizing your business involves more time and effort than simply running it by the numbers. And sometimes that extra effort seems futile. But long term, it has undeniably positive business implications. The success I'm having with EvolveMKD has only reinforced my drive to create a new business model for the public relations and social media industry—one that puts people first.

Launching EvolveMKD was the best decision I ever made—aside from marrying my husband, of course. It has allowed me to live the life I always wanted, even if I didn't know I wanted it at the time. I spend my days working on creative campaigns, tracking statistics and metrics (you can take the girl out of U of C, but you can't take U of C out of the girl), meeting with new and current clients, and fostering a corporate culture that makes the lives of my employees better. EvolveMKD has allowed me to get involved with and behind products that will change the lives of people who use them. Owning EvolveMKD allows me to use my time and money to give back to my community. It allows me to run a business the way it should be run.

Come back in two or three years, and see how we're doing. We'll be waiting for you.

ACKNOWLEDGMENTS

A page isn't long enough to thank everyone whose advice, perspective, and tough love keep me brave and true to my values each day. A few shout-outs:

To my mom, who was the original #girlboss.

To Jonah Shacknai, whose advice, mentorship, and sense of humor make owning a business fun, even on the toughest days.

To my OG clients who helped put Evolve in business: Bill Humphries, Jim Hartman, and Jon Edelson. Thank you!

To my squad of female-CEO pals: Joy, Barbara, Joelle, and all the ladies of the EYWW program. I am so thankful to have you to learn from and be in the trenches with.

To my wonderful team at Evolve, especially my shareholders, Adeena Fried, and Katie "Katherine" Greene. Working with you all and becoming close with many of you is the best unintended benefit of this journey.

Finally, to all the clients that have joined us on this ride. *Thank you!*

ABOUT THE AUTHOR

Megan Driscoll is the founder and CEO of EvolveMKD, a public relations and social media agency based in New York City. She has seventeen years of experience in healthcare, aesthetics and dermatology, and prestige beauty. Key to her success is her ability to always find a way. Megan finds potential in every opportunity for her clients through determination, relationships, agility, and sound strategy coupled with creative spirit. Megan is widely recognized for her work, earning a spot on *PRWeek*'s 40 Under 40 List and being honored as one of twelve women chosen for The Ernst and Young Entrepreneurial Winning Women class of 2018. Additionally, Megan was the first ever recipient of the Early Career Achievement Award from her alma mater, the University of Chicago.

Megan has cultivated relationships with physicians, consumers, key opinion leaders, and tastemakers to gain her clients national level recognition. At the end of the day, Megan wants to surround herself with smart, passionate people who value integrity—people who are serious about their work, but don't take themselves too seriously. This philosophy is at the heart of founding EvolveMKD. At EvolveMKD, Megan provides day-to-day client counsel, strategic direction, and a savvy eye for what makes news and who can make the news happen.

Prior to EvolveMKD, Megan was the President of Behrman Communications, where she managed agency operations, mentored staff, and provided strategic advisement for more than thirty clients. Megan has also held senior roles at Emanate, Lippe Taylor, Fleishman Hillard and Euro RSCG Life PR. When she's not building brands and making media headlines, she's a pasta connoisseur who refuses to operate a moving vehicle. Megan also held childhood aspirations of becoming the president of the United States or a hair stylist. She realized she's settled on a smart compromise between the two.

Megan holds a BA in Public Policy from the University of Chicago.

OUR SERVICES

BRAND CARETAKING

- Brand positioning
- Corporate and Brand Message development
- Physician Relations + Management
- C-Suite message training and positioning
- Identifying + Elevating key partnerships
- Strong background in compliance and regulations
- Global brand launches and activations

CAMPAIGN DEVELOPMENT

- Pre-market conditioning
- Publication plan outreach + Medical meeting communications planning
- Media relations (Traditional + new media, consumer, trade)
- Consumer + Media events
- Spokesperson ID + Training

- Product seeding
- Subscription box partnerships
- Cross-promotional brand partnerships

SOCIAL + DIGITAL MEDIA

- Social Platform Strategy
- Content development + Execution
- Audience development
- Paid media / Ad campaigns
- Community Management
- Social Listening
- Competitive Analysis
- Weekly + Monthly analytics
- Promotional digital activations

INFLUENCER RELATIONS

- Influencer/Blogger Strategy
- Proactive and Reactive Product Seeding
- Paid Partnerships